National The[...]

presents

EXODUS

by Uma Nada-Rajah

C000109312

Exodus was first performed at the Traverse Theatre, Edinburgh,
as part of the Made in Scotland Showcase, on 7 August 2022

EXODUS

by Uma Nada-Rajah

Cast

Asiya Rao	**Aryana Ramkhalawon**
Tobi Tucker	**Anna Russell-Martin**
Haben Haile	**Habiba Saleh**
Phoebe Bernays	**Sophie Steer**
Featuring the voices of	**Lea Shaw** and **Tyler Collins**

Creative Team

Director	**Debbie Hannan**
Set and Costume Designer	**Alisa Kalyanova**
Lighting Designer	**Laura Howard**
Sound Designer/Composer	**Mark Melville**
Video Designer	**Rob Willoughby**
Assistant Director	**Olivia Millar-Ross**
Dramaturg	**Rosie Kellagher**
Casting Director	**Laura Donnelly CDG**

Production Team

Sound and Video Supervisor	**Hana Allan**
Costume Supervisor	**Heather Currie**
Assistant Stage Manager (Rehearsals)	**Reegan Graham**
Lighting Supervisor	**Patrick Hepplewhite**
Company Stage Manager	**Avalon Hernandez**
Assistant Stage Manager/ Tour Deputy Stage Manager	**Katrina McMillan**
Technical Manager	**Malcolm Stephen**
Deputy Stage Manager	**Katie Stephen**
Production Manager	**Elle Taylor**
Costume Technician	**Kathryn Weaving**

Access

BSL Performance Interpreter	**Amy Cheskin**
BSL Performance Interpreter	**Ali Gordon**
Captioner	**Louisa McDaid**
Audio Describer	**Emma-Jane McHenry**

Cast

Aryana Ramkhalawon (Asiya Rao)

Aryana trained at the Guildford School of Acting.

Theatre credits include: *The Funeral Director* (Southwark Playhouse & UK tour), *GH Boy* (Charing Cross Theatre); *The Tempest, Swallows and Amazons, Much Ado About Nothing* (Storyhouse/Grovesnor Park Rep Company); *The Secret Seven* (Storyhouse); *Hijabi Monologues* (Bush Theatre); *Devika, Ode to Leeds* (West Yorkshire Playhouse); *Princess Scintilla* (Nuffield Theatre), *The Secret Garden* (Royal Alexandra Theatre Toronto/Royal Festival Theatre Edinburgh); *Twelve Kali Theatre* (Watermans/ Birmingham MAC/ Rich Mix); *Half and Half* (Welsh Millennium Centre); *The Rose and Bulbul* (Kaddam/Pulse Connects).

For National Theatre of Scotland: *Glasgow Girls* (UK tour)

TV credits include: *Dead Canny* (BBC); *Call The Midwife* (BBC); *Whitstable Pearl* (Acorn TV); *Waterloo Road* (BBC); *Lawless-Drama Matters* (Sky); *Doctors* (BBC); *Crime Stories* (ITV); *Bollywood Carmen* (BBC 3 Live); *Jamillah and Aladdin* (CBBC).

Anna Russell-Martin (Tobi Tucker)

Anna trained at the Royal Conservatoire of Scotland and The Dance School of Scotland.

Theatre credits include: *Life Is A Dream* (Royal Lyceum Theatre); *Nora: A Doll's House* (Young Vic, Citizens Theatre); *Me and My Sister Tell Each Other Everything, Bunny, Colonel Mustard and the Big Bad Wolf* (Tron Theatre); *Cyrano De Bergerac* (Citizens Theatre/Royal Lyceum Theatre/NationalTheatre of Scotland); *A Christmas Carol* (Citizens Theatre); *Toy Plastic Chicken* (Oran Mor/Traverse Theatre).

For National Theatre of Scotland: *The Panopticon*.

TV credits include: *Karen Pirie* (ITV); *Annika* (Alibi); *Casualty* (BBC).

Film credits include: *Falling Into Place, Ghostlight, You Land* (short), *The Shift* (short)

Radio credits include: *KELI, The Portal, Mother Load* (Lepus/Royal Lyceum Theatre), *The Apple, The Tree, Five Days Which Changed Everything, The Kids Table* (BBC).

Anna won a CATS award for Best Female Performance for *The Panopticon* in 2020. She starred in a short film called *The Shift* which has went on to win multiple awards including Best Actress at the Shortez Guimareas Film Festival. This year she received a commended at the Ian Charleson Awards for her performance in *Life Is A Dream*.

Other awards include: Duncan MacRae Memorial Award for Scots Language 2016, and Arnold Fleming Scholarship 2016.

Habiba Saleh (Haben Haile)

Habiba Saleh was born in Cairo, Egypt. Habiba was trained at the American University in Cairo where she graduated with a minor in Theatre Arts.

Theatre credits include: *Magical Plastic Chicken* (Golden Trailer Collective), *Zig Zig* (SHISH VZW) and *Moulin Rouge* (Cairo Opera House).

Sophie Steer (Phoebe Bernays)

Sophie was born in Norfolk and trained at LAMDA.

Theatre credits include: *Civilisation* (Antler/New Diorama), *It's True, It's True, It's True* (Breach Theatre), *Dinomania* (Kandinsky Theatre/New Diorama), *Lands* (Antler Theatre/Bush Theatre), *Still Ill* (Kandinsky Theatre/New Diorama), *Tank* (Breach Theatre/National Tour), *Buckets* (Orange Tree Theatre), *Sparks* (Old Red Lion), *Romeo and Juliet* (Watermill Theatre).

TV credits include: *It's True, It's True, It's True* (BBC4), *Chickens* (Big Talk).

Film credits include: *Days of Bagnold Summer* (StigmaFilms).

Creative Team

Uma Nada-Rajah (Writer)

Uma was a member of the Young Writers' Program at the Traverse Theatre and a recipient of a New Playwrights' Award from Playwrights' Studio Scotland. She is a graduate of École Philippe Gaulier and was recently the Starter Female Political Comedy Writer-in-Residence at the National Theatre of Scotland. She is currently under commission to the Almeida Theatre as a part of the Genesis Almeida New Playwrights Program 2022.

Theatre credits include: *Toy Plastic Chicken* (A Play, A Pie and A Pint – Òran Mór & Traverse Theatre; BBC iPlayer); *The Dubai Papers* (rehearsed reading, Traverse Theatre).

For National Theatre of Scotland: *The Domestic*, *Rapunzel*, *Starter* (Female Political Comedy Writer-in-Residence).

Debbie Hannan (Director)

Debbie Hannan is a new Associate Artist for the National Theatre of Scotland. She was previously Interim Artistic Director for Stockroom, and is directing a short film for Film 4. They trained at the Royal Conservatoire of Scotland and as Trainee Director at the Royal Court.

Theatre credits include: *The Strange Undoing of Prudencia Hart* (Royal Exchange Theatre), *Overflow* (Bush Theatre), *Pah-Lah* (Royal Court Theatre), *Constellations* (Donmar), *Little Miss Burden* (Bunker), *Cuckoo* (Soho) and *The Ugly One* (Tron).

For National Theatre of Scotland: *The Panopticon; Our Ladies of Perpetual Succour* (Associate Director); *Enquirer* (Associate Director).

Alisa Kalyanova (Set & Costume Designer)

Alisa is a freelance theatre designer based in Glasgow. She studied Visual Communication at the Iceland University of the Arts in Reykjavik before training in Set and Costume Design at the Royal Conservatoire of Scotland in Glasgow. Upon graduation she received The John Groves Technical Award for overall achievement. She is an Associate Artist at Brite Theatre company.

Theatre and opera credits include: *Julius Caesar* (Company of Wolves); *hang*, *The Mistress Contract* (Tron Theatre); *Chaos* (Perth Theatre); *Robin Hood* (Cumbernauld

Theatre), *Perkin Warbeck: A Masque of Anamnesis*, *Attempts on her Life*, *The Pool of Bethesda* (Royal Conservatoire of Scotland); *Jamie and the Unicorn*, *Meet Jan Black*, *The Scunner That Stole Christmas* (Ayr Gaiety); *Deliverance* (as creative collaborator, Brite Theatre and Vanishing point); *The Lost Elves*, *Lampedusa* (Wonder Fools); *Humbug!* (Citizens Theatre); *The Trojans* (Platform); *Figaro*, *The Merry Widow* (Opera Bohemia); *Wendy and Peter Pan* (Giggleswick School).

For National Theatre of Scotland: *The Strange Case of Dr. Jekyll and Mr. Hyde* (Costume design).

Laura Howard (Lighting Designer)

Laura is a Lighting and Sound Designer working in the UK and primarily based in London. She trained in Production & Technical Arts at LAMDA.

Theatre credits include: *Cells Out, I Hate It Here* (Camden People's Theatre); *Splintered, Julian and Jules* (Soho Theatre); *Moreno* (Theatre 503); *Dead Air* (Riverside Studios/Stockroom); *Invisible* (Bush Theatre).

Mark Melville (Sound Designer/Composer)

Mark Melville is a composer and sound designer for theatre and film and studied at Leeds Conservatoire. His music and sound design work has been presented across the UK and internationally and exhibited at the V&A Museum, Prague Quadrennial and British Design For Performance festival.

Mark is also a member of the Association of Sound Designers.

Theatre credits include: *Flight* (Vox Motus/The Bridge Theatre/Barbican); *The Metamorphosis* (Vanishing Point/Tron/Emilia Romagna Teatro, Italy); *Byker Audio Stories* (Northern Stage); *A Little Space (*Gecko/Mind The Gap); *Tools For Change* (Theatre Uncut/Traverse); *The Storm* (M6 Theatre); *The Greatest Play in the History of the World…* (Tara Finney Productions/Royal Exchange/West End transfer/UK Tour); *Guards at the Taj, The Children* (Theatre by the Lake); *Frankenstein, Wit, Birth!* (Royal Exchange); *Human Animals; Violence and Son; God Bless the Child* (Royal Court); *1984* (Emilia Romagna Teatro); *Tomorrow* (Vanishing Point/Cena Contemporânea Festival, Brazil/Brighton Festival/Tramway); *Where Do We* Belong?, Where Do We Stand? (Northern Stage); *Little Gift (*M6 Theatre/Andy Manley); *Road* (Leeds Playhouse); *The Manchester Project* (Monkeywood Theatre/HOME); *The Destroyed Room, Saturday Night, The Beggar's* Opera (Vanishing Point); *Charlie Sonata* (Royal Lyceum Theatre); *Wonderland* (Vanishing Point/Napoli Teatro Festival Italia/Tramway/Edinburgh International Festival).

For National Theatre of Scotland: *The Panopticon; Yer Granny; Knives in Hens; Miracle Man; Empty; My Shrinking Life; Dragon (*Vox Motus/National Theatre of Scotland/Tianjin People's Art Theatre, China).

Rob Willoughby (Video Designer)

Rob Willoughby is an artist based in Glasgow who makes theatre, sound and video. He likes to build fantastic worlds and invite audiences to explore them. He is an associate artist with Snap–Elastic, Shotput Dance Theatre and Brite Theatre. He was also the recipient of a competitive micro-commission during lockdown from theatre company Magnetic North to develop his live online video performance practice as *Abbenay2300* on streaming platform twitch.tv.

Theatre credits include: *Ferguson and Barton* with Shotput Dance Theatre, *Me and My Sister Tell Each Other Everything* with Tron Theatre Company, Amy Conway's *Super Awesome World* (Tron/Summerhall), Aby Watson's *This is Not A Euphemism* (Tramway/Buzzcut), Isobel MacArthur's *How to Sing It* (Tron) and Mammalian Diving Reflex's *All The Sex I've Ever Had* (The Arches).

Rob's videography practice has included creating original video content for a variety of clients, including The National Theatre of Scotland (*Playdates – GYOG!*), Snap–Elastic (*Eat Me*), Jordan & Skinner (*A Brief History of the Fragile Male Ego*) and Catherine Wheels (*Whirlygig*).

Olivia Millar-Ross (Assistant Director)

Olivia Millar-Ross is an actor and director based in Glasgow. She trained at Tisch School of the Arts, New York University, and recently graduated with distinction from the University of Glasgow having completed her Common Law (Accelerated) LLB. In 2019 and 2020 she was a Director of Rove St. Productions, a theatre company based in Glasgow.

Theatre credits include: *Either*, *Leopold Vindictive*, *I, Sniper* (Acting Coach Scotland).

NATIONAL THEATRE OF SCOTLAND

WE ARE...

...SCOTLAND'S NATIONAL THEATRE

We tell the stories that need to be told.

...A THEATRE WITHOUT WALLS

We take our work to wherever audiences are to be found. We showcase Scottish culture at home and around the world, telling stories in ways never seen before.

...A THEATRE FOR EVERYONE

We want to break down the walls that prevent people from engaging with our work, whether economic, cultural or physical.

...A CREATIVE CATALYST FOR THE THEATRE SECTOR IN SCOTLAND

Driving joined up talent development plans with partners across Scotland, to nurture theatre makers at all stages of their careers and reflect the diversity of contemporary Scotland.

...ACROSS SCOTLAND AND BEYOND

On the ferry and in the local pub. In the forests and tower blocks. In submarines and swimming pools. On the biggest stages and in the smallest community halls.

The National Theatre of Scotland is dedicated to playing the great stages, arts centres, village halls, schools and site-specific locations of Scotland, the UK and internationally. As well as creating ground-breaking productions and working with the most talented theatre-makers, the National Theatre of Scotland produces significant community engagement projects, innovates digitally and works constantly to develop new talent. Central to this is finding pioneering ways to reach current and new audiences and to encourage people's full participation in the Company's work. With no performance building of its own, the Company works with existing and new venues and companies to create and tour theatre of the highest quality. Founded in 2006, the Company, in its short life, has become a globally significant theatrical player, with an extensive repertoire of award-winning work. The National Theatre of Scotland is supported by the Scottish Government.

Artistic Director and Chief Executive   **Jackie Wylie**
Chair   **Seona Reid DBE**

For the latest information on all our activities, visit us online at **nationaltheatrescotland.com** or follow us on:

National Theatre of Scotland is core funded by

Scottish Government
Riaghaltas na h-Alba
gov.scot

The National Theatre of Scotland, a company limited by guarantee and registered in Scotland (SC234270), is a registered Scottish charity (SCO33377).

SUPPORT NATIONAL THEATRE OF SCOTLAND

Our wonderful donors and supporters help us to:

- Make amazing big shows and wee shows to take all over Scotland, from the grandest theatre stages to the tiniest village halls

- Share stories which reflect the diversity of Scotland – its people, places and history

- Nurture and support Scottish theatre artists

- Reach audiences near and far: on tour, on cinema screens, and across digital platforms

- Create world-class drama and education resources for every school in the country

- Represent Scotland on the international stage

How to support:

- Become a regular Individual Donor

- Corporate Sponsorship

- Introduce us to a Charitable Trust or Foundation

- Remember us in your will

- Attend one of our special fundraising events

Find out more:

Visit **www.nationaltheatrescotland.com/support**

Contact **development@nationaltheatrescotland.com**

Exodus

Uma Nada-Rajah was a member of the Young Writers'
programme at the Traverse Theatre and a recipient of a New
Playwrights' Award from Playwrights' Studio Scotland. She is
a graduate of École Philippe Gaulier and was recently the
Starter Female Political Comedy Writer-in-Residence at the
National Theatre of Scotland. She is currently under
commission to the Almeida Theatre as a part of the Genesis
Almeida New Playwrights programme 2022. Uma also
works as a nurse for NHS Scotland. Theatre credits include
Toy Plastic Chicken (A Play, A Pie and A Pint, Òran Mór and
Traverse Theatre; BBC iPlayer), *The Dubai Papers* (rehearsed
reading, Traverse Theatre), *The Domestic* and *Rapunzel*
(National Theatre of Scotland).

UMA NADA-RAJAH

Exodus

faber

First published in 2022
by Faber and Faber Limited
74–77 Great Russell Street
London WC1B 3DA

Typeset by Brighton Gray
Printed and bound in the UK by CPI Group (Ltd), Croydon CR0 4YY

All rights reserved
© Uma Nada-Rajah, 2022

The opening quotation by Božena Viková-Kunětická appears in
The Literature of Nationalism: Essays on East European Identity,
ed. Robert B. Pynsent (Palgrave Macmillan, 1996)

Uma Nada-Rajah is hereby identified as author
of this work in accordance with Section 77 of the
Copyright, Designs and Patents Act 1988

All rights whatsoever in this work, amateur or professional,
are strictly reserved. Applications for permission for any use
whatsoever, including performance rights, must be made in
advance, prior to any such proposed use, to United Agents,
12–26 Lexington Street, London W1F 0LE (email info@unitedagents.co.uk)

No performance may be given unless a licence
has first been obtained

This book is sold subject to the condition that it shall not,
by way of trade or otherwise, be lent, resold, hired out
or otherwise circulated without the publisher's prior consent
in any form of binding or cover other than that in which
it is published and without a similar condition including
this condition being imposed on the subsequent purchaser

A CIP record for this book
is available from the British Library

978-0-571-38052-7

2 4 6 8 10 9 7 5 3 1

Acknowledgements

Special thanks to Rosie Kellagher at NTS, without whose encouragement, for better or worse, this play would be in the bin. Thank you, Rosie, and also my uncle Martin Robinson, for reading every draft and providing invaluable insight. My heartfelt gratitude goes out to: Debbie Hannan for being fantastic and sound, to Ailie Crerar-Blythe, Jackie Wylie, Anna Hodgart and everyone at NTS for being thorough and wonderful, to my agent Giles Smart and his assistant Ellie Bryne for their warmth and support, to everyone at Faber & Faber, to Joe Farrell for his insight into the politics of farce, to Ella and the profession of nursing for honing my black comedy skills, to Silas Parry, Niall Henderson and Heshani Sothiraj Eddleston for their well-timed encouragement, and to my pals, my housemates and my family: Shantha, Susheela, Shibani, Matt Green and wee Finn Kandiah for everything in-between.

I have my reservations about the notion of a singularly authored text. Thank you to all the actors and creatives who fed into past and present iterations of this script. Namely: Nebli Basani, Charlene Boyd, Emma Callander, Nalini Chetty, Hannah Jarrett-Scott, David James Kirkwood, Camille Marmie, Aryana Ramkhalawon, Anna Russell-Martin, Hiftu Quasem, Gabriel Quigley, Habiba Saleh, Ashley Smith, Sophie Steer, Michelle Tiwo and Kaysha Woollery.

Finally, I would like to express my gratitude to the ecosystem of arts organisations which have nurtured me a playwright, long may they continue to exist and thrive. Namely: The Scottish Society of Playwrights, The Traverse Theatre, Playwrights' Studio Scotland, A Play, A Pie and A Pint, The Kavya Prize and all the public libraries on this planet. This play was written in hope. May we never look away.

Exodus was presented by the National Theatre of Scotland and first performed at the Traverse Theatre, Edinburgh, as part of the Made in Scotland Showcase, on 28 July 2022. The cast was as follows:

Asiya Rao Aryana Ramkhalawon
Tobi Tucker Anna Russell-Martin
Haben Haile Habiba Saleh
Phoebe Bernays Sophie Steer

With the voices of Lea Shaw and Tyler Collins

Director Debbie Hannan
Set and Costume Designer Alisa Kalyanova
Lighting Designer Laura Howard
Sound Designer/Composer Mark Melville
Video Designer Rob Willoughby
Assistant Director Olivia Millar-Ross
Dramaturg Rosie Kellagher
Casting Director Laura Donnelly CDG

Characters

Asiya Rao
Home Secretary, South Asian heritage

Phoebe Bernays
Asiya's special adviser

Haben Haile
asylum seeker trained in the performing arts

Tobi Tucker
journalist, Scottish, working class

Photographer

Conductor

Setting

*The action of the play takes place over a night and a day
in Dover/London.*

EXODUS

'The human being is born in the womb of the nation,
just as the child is born in the womb of the mother.'

Božena Viková-Kunětická

Note

(roman text in brackets) is implied, not spoken

/ indicates overlapping dialogue

Act One

'And the Pharaoh's daughter went down to the Nile to bathe.
She saw the basket among the reeds in the water,
and sent her female slave to get it.
She opened it, and lo and behold she saw the baby.'
Exodus 2: 5–6, NIV

*Dreamscape. Clouds. We are surrounded by water. The
feeling is biblical and camp.*

*Two parallel staircases are suspended from the sky, lit up
in white.*

*As Haben Haile ascends one staircase, she begins to
operatically sing the opening notes to the first verse of 'Rule,
Britannia'. Meanwhile, Asiya, as the pharaoh's daughter/
Britannia, descends from the opposite staircase. She is going
down to the river to bathe. Draped in white linens, she is
resplendent.*

*As the song builds towards the first chorus, a baby in a
Moses basket floats down the centre of the channel. Flashing
lights, the sound of train doors closing, a conductor's whistle:
it is as if an imaginary pink force field surrounds Asiya, a
glimpse of the sense of enclosure in the final scene of the
play. The force field initially repels the baby from reaching
Asiya.*

*At the end of the first chorus, Haben is revealed to have
one shoe on Phoebe's neck.*

7 a.m. Dover. Phoebe's hotel room.

It is the morning after a Tinder date bootie-call. The dregs of a night of drink, drugs and bondage lie scattered against the backdrop of a panoramic view of the White Cliffs of Dover.

Nipple tape is involved. Haben and Phoebe are asleep, intertwined.

Phoebe's mobile phone rings, she gropes around to find it, and eventually finds it and answers.

Phoebe Phoebe Bernays.

Pause.

Yes.

Pause.

Yes.

Pause.

Yes.

Pause.

Noooooooooooooooooo.

With well-honed stealth, Phoebe extracts herself from the bed.
Pause.

I suspect it was made clear to you how important this job is.

Pause.

I don't care what the reason is.

Pause.

And Narinder?

Checks to see if Haben is awake – she is a bit – and whispers down the phone:

I've seen more talent in the aftermath of an enema. You're finished. You'll never work again.

Ends call, smiles politely at Haben, who has now awoken.

Hi.

Haben Is everything okay?

Phoebe Yes. Totally cool. Just. You know. People.

Haben You're cute when you're in a huff.

Phoebe glares.

I mean. People can be difficult. People can make you want to scream.

Phoebe Some people make you want to put your mouth right up to their anus – so you can suck out all their innards and dissolve them in caustic acid.

Haben Hell hath no fury like a woman scorned. Was that a lover on the phone?

Phoebe Oh. No, no. Just work.

Beat.

Yeah. Someone's called in sick.

Beat.

Haben Sorry. What is it that you do for a living?

Phoebe I really should get going.

Haben So soon? Last night. Last night was pretty kinky.

Phoebe (*picking at her nipple*) What is this – ?

Haben Extra-durable nipple tape. I never leave home without it. (*Winks.*)
What's the hurry?

Phoebe I've got to get to work.

Haben Hey. So. Um. Do you. Do you want my number?

Phoebe No.

Beat.

Thanks.

Haben Right. Okay then.
Then what about some coffee? For the road?

Phoebe doesn't answer, she's busy scanning her phone.

I've been in Dover a little while now. Any coffee you find in this place has nothing to do with coffee. See I travel with my own supply. This. This is the real deal. Ethiopia's finest.

Haben shakes the bag at Phoebe. Phoebe gestures, 'Go on, make me a coffee.'

Haben Yes, ma'am.

Phoebe I need to make a call.

Makes a call.

Hi. Lawrence. It's Phoebe Bernays.
Yes. I'm in Dover.

Pause.

I know.
They don't even sell coffee here. I've had to scrounge some off of. a. a.

Smiles at Haben.

Listen. The actor you found pulled out.

Pause. Haben's interest is piqued at the word 'actor'.

I don't know. I don't care. I need you to find me a replacement. Stat.

Pause.

Brilliant.

Pause.

Oh, no no no. No no no. They need to be good to go in less than an hour, from *Dover*. The train leaves from *Dover*.

Pause.

I'd made it perfectly clear to you how important this job is. You need to find me an actor.

Pause. Haben listening carefully to conversation.

Oh, no. That's fine. I understand. And Lawrence?
  Can you do me a favour?
  Yeah. I need you to stop what you're doing and head to your mum's.

Beat.

Yes, your mum's.
  And when she answers the door, what I need you to do is just, crawl back into her vagina, okay? Tell her it might hurt, but it needs to be done, because you've really fucked it as director of communications, and your only real hope is to start again. Right from the very beginning.

Ends call.

Stunning displays of incompetence.

Haben Allow me to cheer you up with some . . . coffee!
  . . . So! I take it you're some sort of famous director?

Phoebe Well, I certainly call the shots.

Haben (*theatrically*) . . . Did I hear you say you were looking for an actor?

More flourish from Haben.

Phoebe (*recalling vaguely*) You're an actor.

Haben This melodic voice. This stunning physique. Could I be anything else?

Phoebe Mmm. You're a bit young for the part.

Haben Oh I've got range, baby. I can play anything from nine months to nine hundred years. (*Winks.*)

And you know I always commit to the cause.

Phoebe What is it you've been in?

Haben Well . . . I'm still under the radar.

Phoebe Good. That's good. That's ideal.

Haben What do you mean, ideal?

Phoebe What if I were to offer you a job? Very well paid. But full non-disclosure.

Haben What does that mean?

Phoebe It means can you keep a secret.

Haben Babes. I'm impenetrable. And for a variety of reasons, a bit of secrecy would suit my current situation.

Phoebe One day's work. Are you free today?

Haben What's the job?

Phoebe Think of it as avant-garde live-action experimental theatre.

Haben MMm. MmmHmm. I have no idea what that is, but I feel I am going to excel at it.

Phoebe This is the role. Steely, understated. The ultimate tragic matriarch.

Phoebe hands Haben a slip of paper. Haben studies it intently. After some time:

Well? Can you do it?

After some time:

Haben This! This is the role I was born to play.

The Dover coastline.
Asiya Rao, poised and expensively dressed, is about to be photographed for an editorial by the Photographer, who is preparing to shoot a few metres away.
Phoebe enters.

Phoebe Home Secretary.

Asiya Oh, there you are, Phoebe! How do I look?

Phoebe What's with the bag?

Asiya It's . . . slimming.

Phoebe It's not, actually.
It makes you look suspicious.

Asiya I like the way it makes me *feel*. (*Gesticulates.*)

Photographer (*calls across the distance*) How are you getting on? I'm ready when you are.

Phoebe (*calls back to Photographer*) Just a minute!
(*To Asiya.*) Give me the bag.

Takes the bag.

Stop slouching.

Asiya stands tall.

(*Loudly to Photographer.*) She needs to have her feet in the water!

Photographer (*calling back over the distance*) She said she doesn't want to!

Phoebe (*to Asiya*) I thought we discussed this.
You're Boudica. Iron-willed. Defending the coast of Britain from siege.

Asiya I know we discussed it, and I like the concept in principle. But –

Phoebe – But what?

Asiya But in reality, the water is quite cold.

. . . To be honest, I think it would have the same effect if I just stood at the edge of the water.

Phoebe You think it would have the same effect if you stood slouching at the edge of the water like some scabrous, diarrhoeic bag lady looking for seashells.

Asiya The bag is Hermès.

Phoebe (*calls to Photographer*) Can you give us a couple of minutes?

Photographer (*calls back to Phoebe*) . . . Well. Actually. The light is perfect right now. I'm not wanting to –

Phoebe – Just. Five minutes.

Photographer But –

Phoebe – Five minutes!

Photographer . . . Right. I'll go and change lens.

Photographer exits in a huff.

Asiya Well now you've gone and done it. He's in a huff. He's going to take a bad photo and make me look fat.

Phoebe Asiya. Look at me. I need you to trust me.

Do you trust me?

Asiya Yes.

Phoebe Big day today.

Asiya Yes. I know.

Phoebe The PM is on his last legs.

This is it. Defining moment of your career.

Nail this interview. And this press conference. And we're going to go all the way.

Asiya Rao for prime minister. Has a nice ring to it, doesn't it?

Asiya It does.

Phoebe I need you on top form.
 Are you on top form?

Asiya Yes. I am on top form.

Phoebe This article is crucial.
 I need you: Poised. Decisive. Oozing leadership material.
 You're Moses. Napoleon. Beyoncé.
 Let's get this image right.
 Asiya Rao standing defiantly against the influx of illegals.
 The bold, refreshing antidote to the paralytic woke
brigade.
 The leader this country so desperately needs.

Asiya I am Napoleon.

Phoebe Yes, Napoleon.
 Now get in the water!

Asiya . . . Maybe I ought to wait till they get back.

Phoebe Now!
 C'mon, Napoleon.

*Asiya hesitates, then does what she's told. Wades into the
water.*

Asiya JESUS FUCKING CHRIST!

Asiya composes herself.

Phoebe That's better.

Asiya practises her 'strong stance'.

Now we're talking!

*Asiya braces herself, looking increasingly statesmanlike.
 After a few moments, a baby washes up near her feet.*

Asiya What on earth is that?

Phoebe . . . I don't know.

Asiya Get it away.

Phoebe What is it?

Asiya Well, it can't be in the frame.

Phoebe Just shove it to one side.

Asiya tries to push it away.

Asiya I can't.

Asiya tries to push it away.

It's following me! It's some sort of . . .
You do it.

Phoebe (*wading in, muttering*) Bloody Napoleon.

Silence.

. . . It's human.

Silence.

Asiya What's wrong with it?

Silence.

Is it (dead) . . . ?

Phoebe I don't know.

Asiya, entranced, reaches out to touch it.

– Don't! –

Asiya, entranced, picks up the baby.

Jesus Fuck.

Asiya It's warm.

Asiya slowly snaps out of her trance.

What should we do?

Phoebe . . . I don't know what to do!

Asiya Well you're a senior adviser.

Phoebe and Asiya stare at each other.
    Rising panic.
    The Photographer re-enters. Closer this time.

Photographer Luckily, the light is still on our side. Let's get cracking.

Reflexively, Phoebe holds the bag open, Asiya shoves the baby in the bag.
    A moment between Asiya and Phoebe.

Photographer Shall we do this? You ready?

Phoebe (*responding to Photographer*) Yes, of course! We were just talking about –

Asiya Zumba.

Phoebe She's ready. She was born ready.

Asiya Yes. Very, very ready.

Hands Phoebe the bag.

Here.

Asiya poses without the bag.
    Photographer hesitates.

Photographer (*calls across the distance*) I prefer it with the bag.
    It makes her look more . . . It's good for her silhouette.

Asiya looks to Phoebe. Phoebe shrugs, reluctantly hands her the bag.
    Asiya stands tall and defiant. The photographer snaps away.

Photographer Brilliant, that's absolutely brilliant.
    These are looking great.
    Perfect. Move your shoulder to the left.
    Chin up towards me, twenty-five degrees.
    Another five degrees.
    Negative-two degrees.

Yes. Yes.
Good. Lift the bag up a bit.
That's nice.

After some time:

Right.
That's us done.

Beat, snaps fingers.

In the bag.

Phoebe What's in the bag?

Photographer . . . It's just an expression.

Phoebe Right.

Photographer I've got what we need.
I'll let you head to the station.

Asiya Wonderful. Thank you!

*The Photographer exits. Some murmurings from the bag,
Phoebe and Asiya in denial of where the sound is coming
from.*

Do you hear that?

Phoebe Hear what?

Asiya That . . . (shrill, high-pitched ringing)?

Phoebe I can't hear anything. It's probably your tinnitus.

Asiya I don't have tinnitus.

Beat.

You really can't hear that?

Phoebe Oh! It's probably my headphones.

Asiya What are you listening to?

Phoebe Opera.

Asiya Opera?

Phoebe I like opera. Just the raw, primal screams of humanity.

Asiya (*hands Phoebe the bag*) You need to get rid of this.

Phoebe What? What am I supposed to do with it?

Asiya I don't know. Put it in a bin?

Phoebe What if someone sees me?

Asiya I know! Leave it with someone with dementia.

Phoebe – But –

Asiya Dover is absolutely riddled with dementia.

Beat.

They'll forget.

Act Two

Minutes later.
A first-class carriage of the 11:05 service from Dover to London St Pancras.
The carriage is at the front of the train. There are two lateral playing spaces: the first-class carriage and a corridor leading to standard class. Asiya stands at a table which will comfortably seat four. The carriage door opens. It's Phoebe. She is breathlessly clutching the Hermès bag. A long pause.

Asiya Did you . . .

Phoebe There was nowhere to –

Asiya I'm surprised. I really am. You're normally so. Efficient.

Beat.

Is it – (dead)?

Phoebe I don't know.

Asiya Well . . . have a look.

Phoebe You have a look!

A stand-off. Neither of them looks.

It hasn't made any – (noises), so it probably is – (dead).

Asiya We need to get rid of it. Leave it in the cloakroom.

Phoebe It's the twenty-first century. There's no 'cloakroom'.
We'll just have to take it back to London and deal with it there.

Asiya (*deep breath*) Right.

Phoebe Right. I need you to focus.
We've not come this far to be put off by a . . . a –

26

Asiya (*mechanically, as in call-and-response*) – a baby.

They look at each other.
Beat.

Phoebe Stick to the core message.
You watch *Britain's Got Talent* and eat a full English breakfast.

Asiya That's disgusting.

Phoebe You're one of them. You want to be prime minister; they need to see you won't go and protect your own.

Asiya Protect my own?

Phoebe Blood is thicker than water, as they say.

Asiya It's actually opposite.

Phoebe What?

Asiya The saying goes: 'The blood of the covenant is thicker than the water of the womb.' Though the origins of that phrase are fiercely debated.

Phoebe (*to Asiya*) Whatever. Focus. You're ruthless. Thunderous. Your balls are bigger, and harder, than any man's.

Asiya My balls are rock solid.

Phoebe But you're feminine. Maternal. Your femininity is the gentle, glissading lubricant that allows us to penetrate the stiff, bureaucratic elites.

Asiya I am lube.

Phoebe You're hard, yet soft. Dominant, yet submissive. Family-oriented, but nothing gets in the way of work.

Haben boards the train swiftly, so very little is given away of her new disguise.

Asiya You're sure this is a good idea? Maybe we should make do without the 'theatrics'?

Phoebe (*unsure*) Of course I'm sure.

Asiya (*re: the baby in the bag*) Given the circumstances.

Phoebe Trust me. We need the actor. An older woman of colour legitimises the entire enterprise. It's a strategic defence, like a pre-emptive counterstrike.

Asiya Okay.

Enter Tobi.

Tobi Hello! Tobi Tucker. Political columnist with *Times on the Train*.
It's a pleasure to meet you.

Asiya . . . Likewise, Asiya Rao.
This is my special adviser Phoebe.

Tobi Phoebe Bernays. Of course.
Your reputation precedes you.

Asiya We are big fans of *Times on the Train*.
'*Times*'! '*On the Train*'! Such an innovative segment.

Phoebe I'm sorry. Who are you ? Where's Scott? I thought this was Scott's piece.

Tobi Oh, erm, Scott's been sacked for sexual harassment.

Phoebe Ah, it's just that we had discussed – in great detail – the concept for this piece with *Scott*.

Tobi I'm afraid Scott is no longer associated with the publication.

Phoebe What is this, bloody call-in-sick Tuesday?

Tobi . . . Erm. He's not sick. He was sacked? For sexual misconduct.

Phoebe 'Tobi Tucker' you say?

Phoebe scrutinises Tobi, then googles her.

Tobi . . . Yeah.

Phoebe (*googling*) Tobi Tucker, political columnist.

Tobi Well, um. I cover a fair bit of style and showbiz . . .

Phoebe Recent articles by Tobi Tucker in the *Times*:
'Top Fifty-Three Matte Lipsticks – Ranked'.
'Top Ten Queer Global Fashion Icons'.
'Are You as Deep as Your Handbag? How to Tell'.
'Hair Rollers: The Return'.
How did you get this gig, Tobi?

Tobi I was in the right place at the right time. No penis.

Phoebe Ah.

Tobi I actually wrote my dissertation on –

Phoebe – Yeah I'm not interested.

Tobi Bennet, our editor, called me personally this morning. He said I should assure you that you were in good hands.

Phoebe . . . Bennet called *you*?

Tobi Yes. He briefed me very thoroughly on what you had in mind for the article. Framing today's big announcement. A bit of background on Asiya. The home secretary's family history. And I mean it's looking like the prime minister has finally patched it – this article will pave your way should you throw your hat in the race.

Tobi mimes throwing a hat, it's awkward.
Phoebe still watching Tobi.
Pause, then:

(*To Asiya.*) – You know, I probably shouldn't say this. But I am a big fan.

Asiya . . . Really?

Tobi It's about time we had a real style icon in the political realm.

Asiya Why, thank you.

Tobi I mean it. Finally, someone, bringing a bit of glamour back into politics.
And can I also say I just LOVE this bag.

Reaches out to touch the bag.

Asiya (*pulling the bag in close*) Thanks.

Awkward silence.

Tobi I can have your story filed before we arrive in London for the press conference.

Phoebe has finished her assessment, Tobi will do.

Phoebe Fine. Let's get started, shall we?

Tobi Oh. Yes. Brilliant.

Conductor (*voice-over*) Good morning, ladies and gentlemen. I'd like to welcome you aboard this direct eleven-oh-five service from Dover Priory to London St Pancras. Your first-class carriage is located at the front of the train.

Your journey time will be approximately one hour and eight minutes, calling into London St Pancras at fourteen minutes past twelve. In the interest of passenger safety, please be advised that all oversized luggage, and larger handheld items, should be placed overhead or on the luggage racks provided.

Tobi I can pop that up top for you.

Asiya I'm sure it will be just fine right here.

Tobi Are you sure?

Asiya hesitates, Phoebe grabs the bag from her and places it overhead.

Phoebe There we go. All tucked up. Safe and sound.

Tobi So. Every *Times on the Train* columnist has their own personal spin on the column. Given the events of the last few days, with the PM on his last legs. What I'd really like to do is get to the heart of who you are as a person. I want my readers to read my column and feel like they've gotten a sense of who you really are. The real Asiya Rao.

Asiya That's lovely. So . . . refreshing. Politics can be so. Dehumanising.

Tobi So. Home Secretary. What gets you out of bed in the morning?

Asiya Greatness. Industriousness. Strength. A sense of duty to the British public. A desire to protect civility. You could say that the greatness of Britain is sewn into the fabric of my psyche. As I'm sure it is in yours.

Tobi Aye. It sure is.
To what do you attribute your success as a politician?

Asiya Well. I suppose it's a bit like showbiz. You've got to give the people what they want. And sometimes, you've got to give people a bit of the ol' razzle dazzle. (*Winks.*) What they didn't know they wanted.

Tobi Could you elaborate on that? What is it that you aim to give people that they didn't know they wanted? I just wondered if you could unpack that for me.

Asiya looks to Phoebe, who shakes her head.

Asiya I love your scarf.

Beat.

Tobi In your time at the Home Office, you have brought about a sea change in British immigration and asylum policies.

Asiya Why thank you, Tobi.

Tobi But what do you say to your critics?

Asiya To my critics, well I just throw them out the window!

Laughs.

I was just being. Humorous.

Tobi To be fair, your policies have been criticised for their violation of international law.

Asiya The British public have given us a mandate to make this nation impenetrable. Nothing goes in, nothing comes out. Everything just stays where it is and festers. In the best way possible. All that's been missing, until now, is the infrastructure.

Tobi The infrastructure. I take it this is your big announcement on our arrival.

Phoebe Yes. We'll get to that.

Tobi Other critics say that your party relies on a culture of fear and mistrust to secure votes. That the tragedies of asylum seekers are being used as a political football.

Phoebe – I've noticed that quite a lot of the *Times on the Train* columns feature a segment on snacks. Why don't you ask the home secretary about what she likes to munch on?

A stand-off. Then:

Tobi (*to Asiya*) Uh. Do you like snacks?

Asiya Funny you should ask. It's been on my mind. My favourite brand of crisps are Ringos. Everyone buys me the new curry flavour, but in fact, I prefer ready salted.

Phoebe mimes 'Write that down'. Tobi reluctantly complies.

I consider myself a great humanitarian.

Tobi You do?

Asiya Britain is, by definition, a humane nation. Anyone that thinks otherwise needs to get with the times. What we need is a bold, new definition of humanitarianism, for a bold, new age. I'm talking about a humanitarianism that works both ways.

Tobi . . . Both ways?

Asiya I'm talking about a 'practical' humanitarianism. It's this bleeding-heart humanitarianism that just defies common sense.

Tobi I'm not clear that we agree on the meaning of that word.

Asiya The meaning of words is a preoccupation of the metropolitan elite. The people of this country are not so concerned with the meaning of words.

Phoebe Like your mum, for example?

Asiya Yes, my mother, for example. Who, unlike yourself, is a woman of colour.

Tobi Okay, uh. Tell me about her.

Asiya My parents came to this country after they were ousted from Uganda in the early seventies. My ancestors had come there from India to help the British run their colonial administration. Uganda was 'The America of the Hindu'. When it all went tits up, my parents came to Britain with nothing. They started from scratch and bought a corner shop. Thatcher herself remarked on how 'entrepreneurial' my parents' generation were. My mum is one of the biggest influences on my life. Manjula is the stiff upper lip personified. She is dutiful, hard-working, reserved. Despite the constraints of my job, I always try to make time for family. When my role as home secretary brought me to Dover, my first thought was: I must bring my mother. She just loves the seaside.

Tobi You brought your mum to Dover?

Asiya I did indeed!

Tobi Well, is your mum here on this train?

A flurry of high-pitched squeals as Haben, disguised as 'Manjula Aunty', bustles her way over to the table. She is an over-the-top Indian-aunty stereotype: oversized glasses, handbag, sari and cardigan, costume jewellery.

Haben (*as 'Manjula Aunty'*) OOOHhhh! Did somebody say my name?!

Phoebe and Asiya look at each other in horror. Perhaps some sex toys are flowing out of Manjula Aunty's bag, which Phoebe covertly attempts to contain.

Asiya OH! Mum?! What on earth are you wearing? It's quite unlike her, this outfit.

Phoebe That wasn't what you were wearing earlier.

Haben (*as 'Manjula Aunty'*) When you said, oh, maybe there will be someone in the media, I got all excited. I will be on camera, no? Look at this. Two ninety-nine. Outrageous. I could have made it at home for nothing. But today, spare no expense. Non no.

Tobi I love what you're wearing!

Haben (*as 'Manjula Aunty'*) She loves it! I love you.

Tobi You must be Mrs Rao.

Haben (*as 'Manjula Aunty'*) Mrs Rao?! Oh! What nonsense these ones. You must call me Manjula. Manjula Aunty.

Tobi It's a pleasure to meet you, Manjula Aunty!
. . . Have we met before?

Haben (*as 'Manjula Aunty'*) No.

Tobi My name is Tobi.

Haben (*as 'Manjula Aunty'*) Tobi. Good teeth. And look at this shirt. Expensive?

Tobi I suppose it was a bit.

Haben (*as 'Manjula Aunty'*) That's a shame.

Pinches Tobi's cheeks.

Chuuku chuuku.
Oh! Disaster! Big big disaster!

Phoebe What's wrong?

Haben (*as 'Manjula Aunty'*) I have forgotten to wear my perfume!

Sprays herself with perfume.

Want some??

She sprays everyone else with perfume, everywhere. Everyone else coughs.

Tobi (*to Asiya*) I thought you said she was reserved.

34

Asiya (*clears her throat*) She is – normally – quite reserved.

Tobi Manjula Aunty, you must be so proud of your daughter. With the PM in such hot water, she may well be the next prime minister.

Haben (*as 'Manjula Aunty'*) My Juju. My jolly Juju. Mummy is so proud of you. So proud.

Tobi Could you tell me what she was like as a child?

Haben (*as 'Manjula Aunty', thinks carefully*) Fat!! Always some kilos too heavy, but what can you do?? Jolly fat coconut. You still love them. Even though. I don't mind a little fat, to be honest with you. Jiggle.

Tobi (*mouths to Asiya*) Omigod I'm so sorry.

Asiya Mothers. What can you do?

Haben (*as 'Manjula Aunty'*) C'mon, smile. Chuuku! Always frowning. What can you do? She's very serious. So serious.

Tobi Asiya was just telling me that you came to this country from Uganda in the early seventies. Can you tell me a bit about your experience of coming here?

Haben (*as 'Manjula Aunty'*) Everything was an utter delight.

Tobi Really?

Haben (*as 'Manjula Aunty'*) Yes.

Tobi Just to be clear, you found the process of migrating here in the seventies to be a walk in the park.

Haben (*as 'Manjula Aunty'*) Why not? The mother country.

Tobi Forgive me for being blunt, but at the time, politicians spoke of 'rivers of blood' to express their unease at the arrival of immigrants from the Commonwealth.

Haben (*as 'Manjula Aunty'*) Who said that? I'll bloody their river.

Asiya My mum is not interested in politics.

Haben (*as 'Manjula Aunty'*) I am not so interested in politics.

Tobi What are you interested in, Manjula Aunty?

Asiya Trains!

Haben (*as 'Manjula Aunty'*) Brown people love trains.

Asiya Vroom! Vroom!

Haben (*as 'Manjula Aunty'*) Sure, built to pillage the wealth of our homelands. But what comfort. What style.

Phoebe Manjula Aunty can't stay with us, unfortunately.

Tobi Oh. What? That's such shame!

Asiya She has lots of knitting to do.

Haben (*as 'Manjula Aunty'*) I hate knitting.

Asiya No you don't.

Haben (*as 'Manjula Aunty'*) It is not in my character to knit.

Phoebe Manjula Aunty just came by to say hello, and maybe she'll chip in later if anything relevant pops up.
Okay. That's enough for now.

Tobi Personally, I'd really love it if you stayed, Manjula Aunty.

Asiya / She can't.

Haben (*as 'Manjula Aunty'*) / I will stay then.
Go on. Ask me anything.

Phoebe and Asiya exchange a look of horror.

Tobi Amazing. This is great. What an honour.

Phoebe You really should rest, Manjula Aunty.

Haben (*as 'Manjula Aunty'*) What is it they say? I'll sleep when I'm dead. And not long to go now.
Very soon. I will be dead.

Tobi Are you . . . Are you dying?

Asiya No. It's just something Indian aunties say.

Haben (*as 'Manjula Aunty'*) Get it while it's hot! Soon it will be a cold cold corpse.

Tobi Manjula Aunty. As a migrant yourself, how do you feel about your daughter's hard-line politics?

Asiya Honestly, she hardly pays attention to politics.

Haben (*as 'Manjula Aunty'*) I hardly pay attention to politics. But for you. (*Winks at Tobi.*) I can waffle on for days. What is this hard-line politics?

Tobi For example, some people have called your daughter's tactics on migration dehumanising.

Phoebe She doesn't have anything to say about –

Asiya – Mummy really doesn't really know about –

Haben (*as 'Manjula Aunty'*) – To take away someone's humanity, my Juju, is always a problem.

Asiya Mummy sometimes likes to play devil's advocate.

Tobi Go on. Pretend I'm not here.

Haben (*as 'Manjula Aunty'*) Humans are humans. Each of us from our mummy's pojaja.

Asiya (*to Haben*) Well, Mummy, I think the fundamental difference between them and us is that we belong here. And we have the documentation to prove it.

Phoebe Manjula Aunty, can I see you for a second?

Haben Civilised people must understand. When the well runs dry, or is flooded or is bombed, one must move along. Juju.

Asiya This well is also running dry, Mummy.

Haben (*as 'Manjula Aunty'*) This well is not running dry. Relatively speaking. People are drawn here by the wealth and civility that this country has plundered from their home nations. My Juju.

Phoebe Aunty?!

Tobi Please go on. This is great.

Asiya The fact is, Mummy. We are a nation under siege.

Haben (*as 'Manjula Aunty'*) You are not under siege, my Juju. The people that come here in their rubber dinghies, they come from siege. Maybe you do not understand 'siege'. I can show you –

Phoebe – Manjula Aunty I must see you in the corridor right now!
    (*To Tobi.*) For her haemorrhoid cream

Haben (*as 'Manjula Aunty'*) Sure, sure, no problem. Everybody wants a piece of Manjula Aunty, what can you do?

    As Phoebe tears Haben away from pinching Asiya's cheeks:

Phoebe Why don't you tell her about some of your hobbies?

Tobi Right then. Tell me what you do to unwind. What do you for fun? Gardening? Zumba?

Asiya To be honest, I think the true moral decline of this country can be traced to the rising popularity of Zumba.

2.2

Tobi nods. The primary action shifts to Haben and Phoebe in the corridor.

Phoebe What on earth do you think you're doing?

Haben Uh, giving the performance of a lifetime.

Phoebe No. You're not. It's awful.

Haben Come again?

Phoebe You are completely missing the mark on this character.
    I thought we'd agreed that you'd stick to the description.

Haben The description? Oh. That was before you gave me the full text.

I have issues with this text.

Phoebe What are your issues with it?

Haben It's badly written.

Phoebe What do you mean it's badly written? I wrote it myself.

Haben Ah. Ah. Ah ha.

Phoebe What's your problem with the text?

Haben 'Manjula Aunty' doesn't make any sense. When you read between the lines –

Phoebe – Your job isn't to read between the lines. Your job is to speak the words on the page.

Haben But I'm a method actor?

Phoebe – Fuck me.

Haben I can't. I'm working.

Phoebe You are being paid. Handsomely. To do a job: Read. The. Words. On. The. Page.

Haben Oh. Oh. Oh! I see there's been a misunderstanding.

Haben starts taking off their costume.

Phoebe What are you doing?

Haben What you want is a sycophant. Some cheap and shoddy two-bit extra from an e-certificate sing-song drama academy. Me? I am an artist. I'm meticulous about my shit.

Phoebe Humans are awful.

Haben What are you going to do, 'suck out my intestines through my anus'? Go on and try. I'll hit you with my handbag.

Phoebe What do you need from me to make this work?

Haben You need to take my process seriously.

Phoebe Okay. Okay.
   Talk me through this character.

Haben Okay. So. It says here: 'Manjula is a strong, reserved, hard-working lady, she has always kept her head down. Her husband has recently passed away.' Then here, in hobbies, it says: 'She has recently taken up Zumba.' See. I think that is a fascinating detail.

Phoebe Don't get hung up on details. I just put that in there because –

Haben – No no no no no! The Zumba detail is EVERYTHING.
   The Zumba moment represents a monumental shift in Manjula's life. I think that in her multiple displacements from India to Uganda to Britain she's been severed from her roots. Until now the grief of this infiltrated every part of Manjula's life. We get the sense her husband was a controlling little fucker. When he died, she found Zumba. I think she's had this transcendent moment at her local community centre. I think she's met this cool group of proper rooted older ladies and now she's coming out of her shell, laughing loudly, speaking in her native tongue. She's going around to the sari shops buying brightly coloured fabrics. I think this is the closest Manjula has ever been to her joyous, authentic self.

Phoebe Okay. That is one potential interpretation.

Haben I am pretty invested in this interpretation.

Phoebe But it's wrong.

   Look of death from Haben.

Okay. It's not wrong. But.

Haben But.

Phoebe But.

40

Haben But.

Phoebe You're saying that this is the closest that Manjula has been to her joyous, authentic self.

Haben That is what I am saying.

Phoebe Well I'm saying. That sometimes. Certain things may be more important than being our joyous, authentic selves.

Haben Come again?

Phoebe Yes. You see. A mother's love conquers all. Asiya wants to be a successful politician. So maybe, for the sake of her daughter's burgeoning political career, Manjula Aunty has taken the decision to set aside her joyous, authentic self, so that she may be seen in the right kind of light.

Haben The right kind of light.

Phoebe The right kind of immigrant.

Haben The right kind of immigrant?

Phoebe A good immigrant. Friendly, but not too friendly. Earnest, but not oppositional. Docile. Hardworking. Grateful.

Haben Like a servant or colonial subject.

Phoebe But modern.

Haben Whoa. Okay. This is a whole other level of – I need to wrap my head around this.

Phoebe I've got a lot to do. I'll leave you to it.

Phoebe goes to exit. Just as she's halfway out the carriage door:

Haben But I am not doing the monologue.

Phoebe What?
You can't not do the monologue.
The monologue is the centrepiece of the entire thing.

Haben The monologue is absurd.

Phoebe You have to do the monologue.

Haben I spent all morning racking my brain. How would Manjula Aunty possibly say something like this? I think there is only one possibility.

Phoebe Yes?

Haben Brain injury. She was hit in the head and developed a severe personality disorder. Half the time she is our warm and engaging Manjula, and half the time she is the sort of cold-blooded psychopath who would speak the words of your monologue.

Phoebe Sure . . . okay. If that's what's going to make it work.

Haben She has this vacant look when she gets into this mode.

Haben pulls an over-the-top 'vacant' face.

Phoebe No! That's not going to work. It needs to feel cohesive. You just need to do the monologue as normal Manjula.

Haben I can't. I don't understand the impulse.

Phoebe Well, here's an impulse.
I'll pay you double.

Haben hesitates.

Triple.

Haben hesitates.

Haben . . . It's still not an impulse.

Phoebe Can I give you a spot of advice? Director to actor.

Haben If you must.

Phoebe It's clear to me that you have some talent.
And it's nice that you have all this artistic integrity.
Or whatever.
But.

Haben But.

Phoebe But.

Haben But.

Phoebe But it's holding you back. Look at you. You don't even have a proper profile.
     Now what I would suggest is that you take your joyous authentic little self and put it on a shelf for a moment and earn some cold hard cash. Or go ahead. Suit yourself. Die an unknown. Writhing around in obscurity, clinging to your precious impulses.

Haben Wait! . . . I'll do the monologue.

Phoebe Good. And be more reserved.
     Think: the Royal Family.

Haben trying out bright and giddy Royal Family waving.

At a funeral.

Haben trying out austere Royal Family waving.

Let's go.

Phoebe and Haben return to the carriage.

Tobi Everything okay, Manjula Aunty?

Haben nods solemnly.

Phoebe Where were we?

Tobi It's been made clear to me that the home secretary does not like Zumba.

Asiya I think of Zumba as a gateway drug. And you know how I feel about drugs! I mean it starts with one Zumba class, but the next thing you know you're face down in the toilet a Berlin nightclub and everyone is dressed as a sexual pony.

The train suddenly jerks forward, and the bag falls from overhead, landing on Asiya's lap.
     Asiya screams.

Tobi Oh, don't worry.
I don't think it's damaged.

Asiya . . . That's a relief.

Tobi takes the bag from Asiya.

Tobi Why don't we put it on the main luggage rack?

Beat.

Oh. It's quite heavy.

Phoebe reflexively snatches the bag out of Tobi's hands.

Asiya That's it. I've had enough.

Haben (*as 'Manjula Aunty'*) Everything okay, Juju?

Asiya It's just that Phoebe's just got her *item* in my bag.

Phoebe My sandwich. It's just my ham sandwich.

Asiya I can't take it any more. Phoebe. I need you to get rid of your ham sandwich.

Phoebe But –

Tobi Your sandwich may start to smell. And it's such an expensive bag.

Haben (*as 'Manjula Aunty'*) Is it?

Tobi Oh, *very*.

Asiya Now! Phoebe.

Phoebe (*to Asiya*) And how would I get rid of it?

Asiya Why don't you just go to a toilet and put it in the bin?

Phoebe I'm sorry. But it's a big sandwich. I don't think it will fit in the bin. It's, um, too big for the bin hole.

Asiya If it's too big, then maybe break it up a little bit.

Phoebe That could get messy.

Asiya (*cracking*) Just do it!! Get rid of it now!

Tobi (*to Haben*) I would be the same way, to be honest. The smell would just start to penetrate. And that's it. Bag ruined.

The baby makes a sound. Phoebe freezes. She yelps to cover it up, looks to exit. A catering trolley is wedged in the corridor, blocking her potential exit.

Asiya Gosh. There's my tinnitus again. Or is it your headphones?

The baby makes another sound. Phoebe makes another sound to cover it up.
Asiya realises the baby is alive.

Tobi (*to Phoebe*) Are you okay?

Asiya (*to Tobi*) She's having an episode. She suffers from . . .

Phoebe sings a note, operatically.

Operatic Tourette's.

Tobi I'm sorry. I had no idea.

Phoebe Nor did I.

Asiya Go on and sing, Phoebe! Sing it out!
(*To Tobi.*) Just the raw, primal screams of humanity.

Haben (*as 'Manjula Aunty'*) Oh! I like to sing opera as well.

Asiya Go on then, Mummy! Sing, come the fuck on and. Sing.

Asiya loudly hums a note to start her off, Phoebe begins to sing 'Ave Maria' to cover up the murmurings from the bag. Haben joins in, takes over; she sings beautifully, a trained voice.

Tobi Your mother's voice is breathtaking.

The song finishes. The trolley from the corridor shifts away.

Phoebe Asiya? Can you please help me with my breathing exercises?

Asiya Give us one moment.

Phoebe and Asiya dash to the corridor.

Tobi That was just beautiful, Manjula Aunty. Your voice is so pure.

Haben (*as 'Manjula Aunty'*) Thank you.

Tobi Something about you feels so familiar.

Haben (*as 'Manjula Aunty'*) Tobi, can I ask you a question?

Tobi Off the record?

Haben (*as 'Manjula Aunty'*) Yes. Let's break the fourth wall.

Tobi You mean the fourth estate. Sure.

Haben (*as 'Manjula Aunty'*) Do you think, Tobi, there is ever any situation in life where one should sacrifice being their joyous authentic self? My daughter and I, we seem to disagree on this matter.

Tobi I'm going to go with no. I think people should always strive to be their 'joyous authentic selves'.

Haben Yes. Exactly. Exactly the fuck right.

Beat; remembers she's 'Manjula Aunty'.

(*As 'Manjula Aunty'.*) My chuuku.

Beat.

What's that look? A flicker of doubt.

Tobi Well. I mean. Sometimes you gotta play the game.

Haben (*as 'Manjula Aunty'*) How play game?

Tobi Maybe you have ambitions. To do something great, you know. Speak truth to power, right some wrongs. But maybe you weren't born with a silver spoon in your mouth. Maybe you've got a fat chunk of debt to pay off and you've gotten stuck writing puff pieces. And all of a sudden you're in the right place at the right time.

Haben (*as 'Manjula Aunty'*) 'If you stare into the abyss the abyss will stare back into you', you know this saying?

Tobi Sometimes you gotta do what you gotta do to get by.

Act Three

3.1

The main playing area shifts to the corridor as Asiya and Phoebe burst in with the baby.

Asiya It's not dead.

Phoebe No.

Asiya I knew it.

Phoebe It actually looks rather healthy. Considering.

Asiya Hi there! Coochie coochie coo!

Baby bites Asiya.

Ow!
It just bit me.

Phoebe Aw, it's got a bit of character.

Asiya What are we going to do with it?

Phoebe I'm thinking.

Baby makes a noise.

We need to keep the baby quiet.

Asiya If you had a bit of tape, you could just –

Mimes 'Tape over mouth'.

I mean it could breathe through its nose.

Phoebe I didn't bring any tape.

Asiya Well that's an oversight.

Phoebe I've got this! Diazepam. We could give it a bit of gentle sedation.

Asiya Yeah. Put it to sleep. Just till we get to London.
You'll have a little nap. Won't you. Won't you?

Phoebe I'm not sure how much to give it.

Asiya Well, it's about half your size. Give it half of what you would take.

Phoebe reads the box, takes out a tablet. Goes to feed it to the baby.

Wait. What if it chokes?

Phoebe Thank you, Mumsnet.

Whips out a water bottle, starts popping tablets into it.

We'll just put some in here, shake it all up and give it a few drops.

Asiya Perfect.

Phoebe Okay! I've got something for you, little one.

Asiya (*cooing*) Yes she DOES! Yes she DOES!

Phoebe tries unsuccessfully to administer droplets to the baby.

Phoebe It's not –
It's just spitting it all back out.
Ow! It bit me.
This thing is feral.

Asiya Well, just.

Phoebe I'm trying!

Asiya Why don't you put a tablet in the other way?

Phoebe The other way?

Asiya Rectally.

Phoebe You put it in the other way.

Asiya tries and fails. A farting noise. The baby shits everywhere.

Asiya It's just done a shit! It's everywhere!
Oh and it smells! Oh!!! OH!!!!

Phoebe – Just shut up and help me clean. One of us needs to go back.

They clean desperately.

Asiya Jesus. Why isn't it wearing a nappy?

Phoebe (*sarcastic*) Yes. Excellent question.
Give me your scarf.

They fashion a nappy/toga out of Asiya's patriotic scarf; they are pleased.

Asiya Coochie coochie coo!
It's actually quite cute, isn't it?

Phoebe Right. You go back out there and act normal.
Get the actor to come in here. We'll have her watch the baby.

Asiya They're a bit over the top, this actor.

Phoebe Just go!

The main playing area shifts back to the carriage as Asiya bursts back in.

Asiya I am SO sorry about that.

Tobi Oh, don't apologise. She's obviously having a really hard time. I'm embarrassed that I've not heard of Operatic Tourette's. But can I just say that it is so admirable that you are genuinely an equal opportunities employer. A lot of people talk the talk but –

Asiya – Well, we do try.

Tobi (*sniffs*) – What's that smell?

Asiya notices a smear of excrement down her sleeve and tries to hide it.

Asiya Oh! Phoebe . . . is also incontinent.

Haben (*as 'Manjula Aunty'*) Is she now?

Tobi With all her talents, I mean, she's such a polymath, I thought, you know, maybe she had some eccentricities. Gosh! I had no idea she was dealing with all of this.

Asiya (*to Haben*) Uh, Mummy.

Haben (*as 'Manjula Aunty'*) Yes, my Juju?

Asiya Phoebe would like to see you in the corridor.

Haben (*as 'Manjula Aunty'*) Little Phoebe wants potty training? (*Winks.*)
   Manjula Aunty can train anything.

Tobi (*to Asiya*) Now, where were we?

Asiya Zumba. See I don't mind people doing exercise, but they should do it in a more restrained fashion.

The main playing area shifts back to the corridor as Haben bursts in.

Haben I didn't know that we would be singing opera! Opera is my greatest passion.

Phoebe, now pretending to be an avant-garde theatre director, is turned so Haben cannot yet see the baby.

Phoebe Did you say to me that you were an artist?

Haben Yes.

Phoebe . . . A *real* artist?

Haben Of course.

Beat.

Phoebe Then prepare to meet your new teacher!

Turns around to reveal the baby.

Haben What's this? A baby?

Phoebe In my experience, actors – and method actors in particular – tend to get bogged down in the backstory. But babies. Babies are eternally in the present.

This baby is your teacher.

Haben My teacher.

Phoebe I want you to study the baby. In silence.

You must keep this baby calm, and quiet. Under no circumstances will you come back into the carriage, unless instructed to do so by myself or Asiya.

Do you understand the exercise?

Haben Yes. I understand.

Phoebe You will learn to be present.

Haben (*studying the baby*) 'The baby is eternally in the present.'

Beat.

Wait. Where did this baby come from?

Phoebe Repeat after me: 'The backstory.'

Haben 'The backstory.'

Phoebe 'Is inconsequential.'

Haben 'Is inconsequential.'

Wow. Wow! I once read about this theatre director in Poland who would take his actors to run around with the wolves and the bears, to release their inner wildness.

But, babes. This is some next-level shit right here.

Phoebe I am wasted in Westminster.

Beat.

Haben Can I ask you a quick question? This is probably . . . I'm probably misunderstanding the genre.

Phoebe Sure.

Haben This 'live-action experimental theatre' . . .

Phoebe Yes?

Haben . . . That's not the real home secretary. You know what, I'm just gonna go on and google her.

Phoebe (*hesitates*) That is the real home secretary.

Beat.

Haben Erm. You said this job is cash-in-hand?

Phoebe Yes.

Haben I'd like to cash out now please.

Phoebe What?

Haben Cash please.

Phoebe I don't carry cash. No one carries cash.

Haben You said cash-in-hand.

Phoebe It's just an expression.
    You can't leave now.

Haben I really should. I am in the process of seeking asylum due to persecution in my home country on account of my sexuality.

Phoebe Fuck me.

Haben That would be inappropriate. I like you, Phoebe. We may have our artistic differences – I don't get you with that monologue. But despite all this, I find your dedication to this strange art form . . . fascinating. When I look at you. I feel alive. You know there are people in my country, who have tried to kill me for this. Simply because looking at your collarbone makes me feel alive. Violent thugs, what business is it to them, I don't know. I have had to flee my country, in fear of my life, because of who I am. And I have only been here a short while, but already I have had a night of passion beyond my wildest dreams, and I am working as an actor in a genre I didn't even know existed! This country is a beacon of light. It is a land that is celebratory and diverse, a place of openness and curiosity, a nation reckoning with its past. This is a land of great literature and drama, where words have meaning, and people are rigorous in their attention to detail. It is a land where people have fought against tyranny and closed-mindedness, not just for themselves, but for others. It is a place of decency and humanity. This is where I want to live. This is where I want to tread the boards. If that is the real home secretary. The best thing is for us to settle the score and I'll be on my way.

I have a good case. A clean case. A clear-cut case.

I do not wish to jeopardise my claim.

Phoebe The only thing that would jeopardise your claim is if you walked away from me right now.

Haben I'm going through the proper channels.

It's a straightforward, legitimate case.

Phoebe I'm sure you are. And it just got a hell of a lot *more* legitimate.

Beat.

I imagine you would like it to *stay* legitimate.

Haben But –

Phoebe Do you understand what I'm trying to say?

Haben Yeah. I think I do.

Phoebe Now, when you are called back in. You will recite the monologue verbatim. Do you understand?

Haben . . . I understand.

Phoebe Very well.

The main playing area shifts back to the carriage as Phoebe heads back for the table.

Tobi (*to Phoebe, patronising*) Can I just say? I think you are so brave.

Phoebe Thank you.

Tobi . . . Would you like some hand sanitiser?

Phoebe Uh. Sure.

Phoebe sanitises her hands.

Tobi And what about some body spray?

Phoebe Uh, no. I'm all right.

Asiya Go on, take some, Phoebe!

Phoebe Sure. Go on then.

Phoebe gets doused in body spray.

Asiya It's the twenty-first century, Phoebe! It's okay to be incontinent!
I'm very much a progressive.

Tobi Phoebe, and obviously this is all off the record, I had no idea what you've been going through. From the outside, you're seen as this mastermind, a polymath, Phoebe Bernays, of the great Bernays family, pioneers of British engineering. You seem so composed, almost too composed. To be honest, it's just good to know that you're human.

Phoebe Well, I do what I can to put on a façade. But inside, it's all . . . opera!

Tobi I've had a tiny bit of depression myself. But you. You are an inspiration.

Phoebe Thank you. Now. Let's get back on track.

Tobi You were about to tell me about this afternoon's big announcement.

Asiya It's all terribly exciting. British innovation at its finest.

Phoebe Come to think of it. I'm glad Scott's not here.

Tobi Oh?

Phoebe Because he wouldn't have appreciated some of the nuances of this new project the way that you will. Being a woman. A feminist?

Tobi Of course.

Phoebe What comes to mind when you hear the word 'womb'?

Tobi I'm sorry?

Phoebe An enclosure of independence. An encapsulation of freedom. A cellule of sovereignty.

Asiya We have been called upon to defend the sovereignty of the mother country.

Phoebe At the Home Office we have been having very exciting discussions with a number of British tech companies.

Asiya Tremendously exciting. God. I feel so alive just thinking about it.

Phoebe We present to you: Project Womb.

Asiya We are going to create a wall of ionising radiation to surround the whole of the British Isles.

Phoebe Like a womb.

Asiya A thermonuclear womb!

Phoebe whacks Asiya.

Thermowomb. Thermowomb. A bold, new border for a bold, new age. A network of interconnected blimp drones emitting high-frequency ionising radiation on detection of any form of life.

Tobi What will happen to people if they come into contact with –

Asiya – Nothing. Nothing would happen to anyone. It's a deterrent. A thermonuclear . . . thermodeterrent.

Tobi What about the fish?

Asiya There have been some minor hiccups. The British fish are, for the most part, delighted.
It's foolproof.

Tobi What could possibly go wrong?

Asiya Not only does it address the migrant invasion: No dinghies shall pass! By surrounding the British Isles in their entirety, we'll have a de facto solution to the whole issue with . . .

Snaps her fingers, trying to remember.

Phoebe – Ireland.

Asiya Yes, Ireland.

Tobi You're going to annex Ireland?

Asiya And even solves the issue with your people.

Tobi Scotland?

Asiya Unify the isles. One nation under wall.

Tobi I don't think that's going to go down very well.

Phoebe – It is the sort of infrastructure that really brings people together.

Tobi tries to get a word in, but can't.

Asiya
'– Sound the loud timbrel o'er Egypt's dark sea!
Jehovah has triumph'd – His people are free!
Sing! for the pride of the tyrant is broken,
His chariots his horsemen all splendid and brave,
How vain was their boasting! The Lord had but spoken.
And chariots and horsemen are sunk in the wave.'

Tobi Can I just clarify, the people sunk in the wave are the –

Asiya Migrant invaders.

Phoebe Yes.

Tobi Ah, okay, so you are the chosen people.

Asiya (*flattered*) Well, it's just an analogy, but.

Tobi . . . In this analogy, you are the undocumented destitute, deprived of land and status.

Asiya Well . . .

Tobi I'm lost . . . Are you the pharaoh, or the Israelite enslaved?

Phoebe Well, funnily enough, she's both. Her mother. Came here with nothing.

Asiya Absolutely nothing. But do you know, one of the biggest advocates for technology like this will be my mother?

Tobi Manjula Aunty? Really? That would really surprise me.

Phoebe Well then let's hear it from the horse's mouth.
   I'll go and get Manjula Aunty.

Tobi You two have been running about so much. I'll go and get her.

Phoebe (*jumps up and shouts*) No!!

Asiya I'll go!

   Beat.

I love my mummy.

   Asiya heads to corridor.
      The main playing area shifts to the corridor. As Asiya enters, the baby is just drifting off to sleep as Haben rocks her gently.

Asiya You need to go and do your monologue.

Haben Ah, the baby is just about to fall asleep.

   Rocking the baby to sleep, singing to it. Perhaps they sing all their lines in this section.

Asiya Right then, get it to sleep first. That would be best.

Haben speaks sofly, gently rocking the baby to sleep.

Haben It's a beautiful name, Asiya. Asiya, who found the baby in the water.

Asiya . . . She told you about that?

Haben It's in the Bible.

Asiya What?

Haben The Book of Exodus. Asiya is the name of the pharaoh's daughter.
You don't know this story?

Asiya Just get the baby to sleep.

Haben Once upon a time, there was a great battle between the gods and the kings, and ordinary people were caught in the crossfire. The pharaoh is a tyrant. He declares that all firstborn sons of Israelites should be slain. But Moses' mum isn't having it. She bundles her baby into a basket and floats it across the Nile, just across from the gates to the palace. And as Asiya, the pharaoh's daughter, goes down to the river to bathe, she sees the basket in amongst the bulrushes and sends her little maiden lady to get it. They look down and lo and behold, they see a baby! Asiya gives it sanctuary. Moses is taken into the palace and raised as one of their own. He is given the keys to the kingdom, only to lead an exodus and revolt. They say one's name is one's destiny. Asiya. Your destiny is to nurture the leader of the revolution.

Asiya Revolution?! I'm not interested in any such thing.

Haben Shhh! The baby is asleep!

Asiya (*grabbing the baby*) Great! It's asleep! Go go go! It's time for your monologue.

Haben exits to the carriage. The baby begins to stir with Asiya's furious rocking. The main playing area shifts to the carriage as Haben goes to take her seat.

Tobi Manjula Aunty!

Haben (*as 'Manjula Aunty'*) Yes, I'm back.

Tobi The home secretary was just telling me that you are in support of a directed energy sea wall around the British Isles. I'm really interested to get your take on it.

Haben (*as 'Manjula Aunty'*) I would like to go on the record to say that I am utterly in support of Project Womb.

We must maintain our borders at all costs. We must protect our own. We must provide for our own. 'The human being is born in the womb of the nation, just as the child is born in the womb of the mother.' Do you know this saying? The trials and tribulations of others are not for us to bear. Our rights and freedoms are for us alone. Concern for the plight of others is taxing. We should be shielded from such concerns by the state, as the mother protects her child from the outside world. I like this analogy of the womb, as it is the ultimate comfort. Safe and secure, nothing goes in, nothing comes out. All there is for us to do is shut our eyes and think of nothing but ourselves and our own. We are lulled to sleep to the rhythm of the steady beat of nationhood, enclosed in the warmth of soft, pink tissue.

The sound of the baby crying in the corridor.

Tobi Is that a baby crying?

Phoebe No! That's Asiya's mobile! It's her ringtone from Number Ten.

Now the two of you stay exactly where you are.

Phoebe exits to corridor.
The main playing area shifts back to the corridor as Phoebe enters. The baby is now awake and crying.

Phoebe You need to keep it quiet!

Asiya I know. What's it doing? It keeps knocking its head against my chest.

Phoebe It wants to feed.

Asiya Oh! That's disgusting.

After some time:

Do you think I should let it feed?

Phoebe Well, if it shuts it up.

Asiya (*to herself*) Well. All right. Okay. What is that quote about breastfeeding?
'Come to my woman's breasts and take my milk for gall'!

Asiya hesitantly lets her bra down so the baby can feed at her breast.

Look at this creature. Wonderful. It's just pure. Instinct.
Ah! It's biting me. / Ow. Ow.

Phoebe (*pacing*) Everything is, more or less, going according to plan. She's got the quote.
All we need to do is keep that thing quiet and get off this bloody train.

Asiya Yes, things seem to be going quite well, considering. OW!

Phoebe Shh!

Asiya Phoebe.

Phoebe Yes?

Asiya Do you think I'll ever land the top job?

Phoebe Yeah. Of course.

Asiya Okay, it's really nipping now.

Suddenly the baby bites off Asiya's nipple.
   Asiya screams.

Phoebe What? What's wrong?

Asiya My nipple.

Phoebe What?

Asiya It's come off. It's been bitten off.

Phoebe Don't exaggerate.

Takes the baby from Asiya. Looks at her nipple.

Oh God.

Asiya It's . . . It's dangling. There's a lot of blood.

Phoebe Asiya, look at me.

Asiya It hurts.

Phoebe Do you or do you not want to be prime minister?

Asiya I only have one nipple.

Phoebe Look, you're going to have to harden the fuck up. Can you do that?

Asiya (*shakily*) Yes.

Phoebe Pull yourself together.

Asiya I need to sit down.

Phoebe (*hands Asiya a garment of some sort*) Just put some pressure on it.
Look at me. Who do you admire?

Asiya Thatcher? Napoleon? Beyoncé?

Phoebe You've got a tiny little battle wound.
What would Beyoncé do?

Asiya I don't know.

Phoebe She's a survivor.

Asiya woozily sings the chorus of Destiny's Child's 'Survivor'.

Take the baby.

Asiya, now a bit frightened of the baby, keeps singing as Phoebe talks over her.

Pull yourself together. I'm going to go out there and wrap it up. Okay? And then I'll be right back. You stay. Right. Here.

The main playing area shifts back to the carriage as Phoebe enters and heads for the table.

Tobi, I am terribly sorry. But I'm afraid we're going to have to wrap things up.

Tobi What? We were just getting into it.

Phoebe Home Secretary must deal with an urgent matter.

Tobi I have so many more questions. I can wait –

Phoebe No. That will be all.
Let's quit while we're ahead, shall we?

Asiya, bloodied and disorientated, stumbles into the corridor holding the baby. She collapses.

Act Four

4.1

Dreamscape. We are inside Asiya's unconscious. We are at sea. Winds and rain, but the rain is made up of tiny bottles of hand sanitiser. Beyoncé's 'Halo' plays. Perhaps the others dance a slow Zumba routine. The baby in the basket (as in the opening scene) floats past. She picks up the basket and has a transcendent moment with it. Lights dim as the song winds down and we hear:

Phoebe Asiya?

Tobi Hello? Hello?

Phoebe Asiya, can you hear me?

4.2

Lights come up on Tobi and Phoebe standing over Asiya and fanning her awake.
  Haben is holding the baby.

Phoebe Asiya, can you hear us?

Tobi She's coming to!

Phoebe Thank God.

Tobi Where on earth has this baby come from?

  Silence. Asiya and Haben and Phoebe look at each other.

Asiya (*suddenly alert*) It's mine!

Tobi What?

Asiya The baby is mine!

Tobi It is?

Phoebe Yes . . . yes . . . yes!!! Of course it is!!

Phoebe gives Haben a look.

Haben (*as 'Manjula Aunty'*) Oh, my grandchild! My grandchild is my teacher.

Tobi . . . Ah!! I see! All of this is all starting to make a lot more sense.

Haben (*as 'Manjula Aunty'*) Is it now.

Tobi This explains so much. The erratic behaviour. The recent mood swings.
. . . The pregnancy weight . . .

Asiya Do you know? It's been hard to shake the pregnancy weight, but of course, I've had other things on my mind.

Tobi Does it not wear nappies?

Phoebe It's free range.

Asiya You know, despite all her troubles, Phoebe is a great help with the care of the baby. And of course, this is the real reason my mum came to the seaside with me.

Pause.

Tobi I feel like I owe you both an apology. Wow. Women are amazing. Women.
I came into this with a lot of preconceptions of what both of you were like, but here you are, quietly juggling caring roles as women. I had you pinned as just another power-hungry narcissist and her Machiavellian spad. But all that time, you were trying to cover for each other, supporting each other, through the ups and downs, as working women in caring roles.

Asiya Thank you. Thank you very much.

Phoebe and Asiya beam at each other.

Tobi What's its name?

Asiya . . . Momo!

Tobi Oh.

   Beat.

That's nice.

Haben (*as 'Manjula Aunty', whispering to herself*) Moses.

Phoebe It's, uh, traditional.

Tobi What's the spelling of that?

Phoebe We would like to keep the baby off the record.

Asiya I want to protect my child from the daggers of the public eye. You understand.

Tobi Of course. Of course. Quite a sacrifice to make. I'm impressed.

Phoebe What do you mean?

Tobi Just that it would bode so well for your image.

Phoebe Yes!

Tobi I'm no . . . strategist. That's your domain. But you're that heady mix – woman of colour from a working-class background with your hard-line conservative politics – also a single mother. With the prime minister about to patch it. I mean, come on . . . It's twenty-first-century political dynamite. I'm sure you've mulled this over already. And I do think that it's so highly commendable that you just want to do what's in the best interest of the child.

Phoebe We had mulled it over, Tobi. And we were torn.

Asiya Incredibly torn.

Phoebe So torn. And it's especially difficult, seeing as you seem to really understand the essence of who we are as women, and as politicians.

Tobi Of course! Originally, this was Scott's article.

Phoebe And Scott just wouldn't have really *got it*.

Tobi He really wouldn't have.

Asiya But Tobi.

Phoebe Tobi really seems to *get it*.

Tobi This is exactly what I'm all about right now. Women, women in caring roles, intergenerational politics, motherhood. It would be such a great angle for the column.

Phoebe We were so set against it.

Asiya But. The truth shall set you free.

Phoebe And you are a big fan of the truth.

Asiya I am a big fan of the truth.

Phoebe You have our permission to include Momo in the article.

Tobi What an incredible story! A top contender for prime minister is a single mum! The inside scoop on the inspiring feminist support network behind it all!

Phoebe Please don't use the baby's first name.

Tobi Of course not.
   (*To Asiya.*) Tell me, Home Secretary, has motherhood changed your political views?

Asiya Motherhood has only fortified my political standpoint. What if little Momo doesn't have a place at school or misses a life-saving operation because of some illegal refugee? Now that would just break my heart.

Phoebe Momo's arrival was the real inspiration for Project Womb –

Haben (*as 'Manjula Aunty, looking at Asiya's chest*) – Sorry to interrupt. But you are bleeding heavily.

Asiya Oh that, it's just a breastfeeding injury.

Phoebe Her nipple popped off.

Tobi Popped off? Is that a thing?

Asiya Happens all the time.

Phoebe But like the stories of so many women, oft goes untold.

Haben (*as 'Manjula Aunty'*) I've got some extra-durable nipple tape. I never leave home without it. (*Winks.*)

Phoebe Manjula Aunty is always prepared.

Haben Let me see . . . Ugh!

Tobi You must be in so much pain.

Asiya I do not feel pain, only love for my child.

Tobi Aw, that's beautiful. What were you saying about the strategies that Momo has inspired?

Haben uses the tape to patch Asiya's nipple back on.

Phoebe Project Womb was conceived around the time of Momo's birth. The home secretary felt a renewed sense that we must, as a nation, prioritise British babies like Momo. Project Womb will demand a radical re-enforcement of immigration and asylum policies, drones, deep surveillance technology, directed-energy weapons, razor wire, sniffer dogs . . .

Haben makes an 'error', Asiya screams in pain.

Asiya OWWWWWWW!!

Haben (*as 'Manjula Aunty', smiles politely*) That's it all done.

Tobi's phone rings.

Tobi If you'll excuse me. It's Bennet. My editor.

Tobi exits to the corridor.
Asiya begins to develop a bond with the baby.

Haben (*as 'Manjula Aunty'*) Well. This has been interesting. Maybe this is a good time to part ways.

Phoebe Yes. Fair enough. I'll be in touch to arrange what was promised to you.

Haben (*as 'Manjula Aunty'*) Yes. About that. I'd like some collateral.

Phoebe You have my word.

Haben raises an eyebrow.

Haben (*as 'Manjula Aunty'*) Yeah. I'd definitely like some collateral.

Phoebe Right. Okay. This is an authentic Hermès bag. Worth thirty-eight thousand in its current condition.

Asiya (*to the baby*) / Coochie coochie coo! Oh it's just adorable.

Haben (*as 'Manjula Aunty'*) / And you went and put your ham sandwich in it? Dear God.

Phoebe / You can air it out. Stick it out the window in the corridor. By the time we get to London it will be fresh as a daisy.

Asiya (*to the baby*) Oh. Aren't you just the cutest?

Phoebe Hey. Uh, listen. If you're ever in London –

Haben (*as 'Manjula Aunty'*) Uh, I think I might steer clear of online dating.

Haben exits with the bag. Tobi passes her in the corridor.

Tobi Everything all right, Manjula Aunty?

Haben (*as 'Manjula Aunty'*) Just going to get some air.

Tobi Fair play.

Haben, cradling all Manjula Aunty's props, passes Tobi in the corridor and nods.

Sorry about that.

Phoebe No problem.

Tobi Bennet was wanting to know if I was still in Dover. There's been some breaking news.

Phoebe What's happened?

Tobi A dinghy that had been carrying migrants has capsized near the coast. The lifeboats are all out scouring the water. It was close to where you were for your photo shoot, funnily enough.

Phoebe and Asiya exchange a look.

So far, no survivors have been found. A report from Calais says there was a baby aboard. A baby. Can you imagine? There is a photo circulating of the lost baby. It was taken with Mum before fleeing their homeland. He has these big, bright beautiful eyes.

Tobi looks over at Momo, Asiya pulls Momo in close.

God. It's heartbreaking. Let me get the photo up.

Asiya No!

Phoebe Please don't be gratuitous.

Asiya Have some decency. There's no need for that. It's too much.

Phoebe pinches the baby, making it cry.

Phoebe – Look, Tobi. I hate to be rude.
    But Momo is distressed? Maybe you could make yourself useful?

Tobi Uh. Yes. Of course. What can I do?

Phoebe Milk. We need milk. Go to the café car and get us a bottle of milk.

Tobi Bottle of milk. Got it.

Phoebe With a teat!

Tobi Uh, a teat? . . . What if they don't have a teat?

Phoebe Just get one of those sport water bottles and put some little portions of milk in it?

Tobi Oh right. Of course.

Beat.

Uh. How many milks?

Phoebe About forty-two.

Tobi Forty-two.

Tobi takes a long hard look at Momo. Exits.

Asiya What are we going to do? There's a photo!

Phoebe (*pacing*) Could we disguise it somehow?

Asiya Yes! Yes! Momo is a bit dark. I mean, for it to be mine. I mean he is beautiful, and I do see the resemblance, but I'm quite fair. Give me your foundation.

Asiya runs some pale foundation across the baby's face.

Ugh! This isn't working.

Phoebe Could we own it?

Asiya Own it?

Phoebe We say we found the baby. Rescued the baby. A sunken dinghy means, the grounds have shifted. It could make you seem . . . humane.

Asiya Of course. We could say that I reached into the water this morning, like some sort of great Earth Mother saved it. We could redo the whole photo-shoot – I'd have this beautiful glow.

Phoebe But what would we say you were doing with the baby?

Asiya We could say I was taking it with me to be interviewed. We could say I was taking it with me so that it could be thoroughly vetted through due process.

Phoebe Due process. People love that.

Beat.

We didn't do that. We ought to have handed Momo over to the police.

Asiya Watch your tone!
(*Protectively.*) Momo is not a criminal.

Phoebe Momo entered British waters illegally.

Asiya How dare you insult my child?

Phoebe We ought to have dealt with it then and there. We can't own it.

Asiya Then what are we going to do?

Phoebe What we ought to have done miles ago. We need to get rid of it.

Asiya What? We can't just get rid of it. This is my baby.

Phoebe This is not your baby. You plucked it out of the sea. It needs to go.

Asiya But. It's. (Human.)

Phoebe I know. But. It can't be. That.

Asiya It's my baby. It's a baby.

Phoebe I know it seemed like a baby. It can no longer be a baby. Everything that we stand for depends on this not being a baby. Greatness involves sacrifice.

Asiya Sacrifice.

Phoebe Your job. Your calling is to defend this soil. This baby. Is a threat to our sovereignty.

Asiya But it's just one.

Phoebe But where does it end?
Do you want to be living in a mud hut?

Asiya I don't like the mud.

Phoebe 'Earth Mothers' sounds nice in theory, but in reality it's a bunch of mud-streaked toddlers of indeterminate lineage, running feral in itchy grass.

  Beat.

If there is one defining characteristic of our party, it is that we *endure*. And we do what needs to be done, to continue to endure. This is survival.

Asiya Do you think people like me?

Phoebe They may not like you. But they respect you. You have the courage to do what they cannot.
  You're going to be the next prime minister.

Asiya It's just a cluster of cells.

Phoebe Sure.

Asiya If I've gone on record as being a mum, I'm going to need a baby.

Phoebe We'll source another one.

Asiya From where?

Phoebe Calais, Lampedusa, Lesvos.

Asiya And we'll give *that* child a better life.

Phoebe Yes.

Asiya This one was –

Phoebe Yes this one was already –

  Phoebe goes to the window, opens it, looks outside.

Fields. Just fields.

  Beat.

Well?

Asiya 'Tis better to be feared than loved.

Asiya closes her eyes and chucks the baby out the window.
A dull thud.

   Asiya and Phoebe look at each other. The sound of the
train along the tracks.

4.3

A shift in tone.
   Asiya and Phoebe are sat in silence.
   Sounds of the train. Tobi re-enters the carriage holding a
sports water bottle and forty-two individually packaged
milks. She pours the packets into the bottle methodically.

Tobi . . . I've got the milk. Where's Momo?

   Pause.

Phoebe Momo has gone for a sleep.

   Beat.

A big sleep.

   Tobi shoves the milk parcels to one side.

Tobi They've still not found any survivors. And there's no
clear estimate of how many were aboard that dinghy. It's
unimaginable. For some babies, no expense is spared to
preserve their lives. And for others, the Coastguard is ordered
to turn back. They are left to drown. Their lives are a burden.
Not worth the hassle. Unwanted, undesirable, untouchable
from birth.

   Beat.

Who are we, as a people, if we can't acknowledge the
humanity of a child seeking refuge? What have we become?
You'll know as well as I do, it's moments like this where the
entire context shifts. All it takes is one photo of a baby,
drowned at sea. And the entire nation will stop in its tracks.
   When that photo surfaces –

Phoebe – Yeah, that's not going to happen.

Tobi ?

Phoebe That is not going to happen – in the future. Because. Our official comment from the Home Office is that this is exactly why the Project Womb is being put in place. To prevent tragedies such as this from occurring. In the future.

Beat.

God. I am parched.

Phoebe chugs the contents of her water bottle, not realising it's the diazepam water. Okay. Now Phoebe realises.

Tobi With all due respect, I'd like to hear directly from the home secretary.

Asiya Was tha . . . Momo? Never mind. Sorry. I just thought I'd heard Momo.

Tobi . . . Right.

Asiya Is it coming from out in those fields?

Phoebe Oh that. That must be my. Uh. Headphones.

Tobi You're not wearing any headphones.

Phoebe Momo has gone for a sleep, remember?

Asiya Yes. Momo has gone for a sleep.

Beat.

Of course.

Tobi May I have an official comment, Home Secretary?

Phoebe (*starting to get drowsy*) Maybe just give it a rest. Maybe we should all just take a rest?

Sometimes I feel like it's all just go go go. Go go go. Win win win. Win all of the things. And for what? Where are we going? What is even the point? What is even on the other

side? What would happen if we stopped? That would be bad.
Oh no. That would be really bad.

*Asiya clocks Phoebe's drowsiness. Notes the water
bottle.*

Asiya Phoebe! Pull yourself together!

*Asiya slaps Phoebe across the face. Phoebe regains
coherence.*

Do you not hear that?

Tobi stares in shock at both of them.

Tobi Is everything okay?

Asiya Oh. Nothing to worry about.
Just a little thing we do. Slip slap.

Phoebe So empowering.
Coffee. I need coffee.
(*To Asiya.*) Be nice! She's right . . . 'the context has
shifted' . . .

*Phoebe drowsily exits via the corridor. Through the
following exchange, Phoebe stumbles past Haben in the
carriage, slapping herself, focused on going to buy
multiple espressos from the café car.*
Tobi hones in on Asiya.

Tobi I think people would like to hear from you, Asiya, at
this moment in time, as a potential future leader of this
country. Unless of course the demands of motherhood are
just too onerous to address the nation. Which is totally,
totally understandable.

Asiya I may be family-oriented, but nothing gets in the way
of work.

Tobi Fantastic.

Beat.

Asiya It's silly. But sometimes I miss Momo even when he's . . . sleeping.

Tobi Don't apologise. It's unexpected. If you want my honest opinion, these deeply maternal emotions make you all the more relatable.

Asiya brings her hands to her face and inhales.

Asiya I can still smell him. 'All the perfumes of Arabia will not sweeten this little hand.'

Tobi What if that were your baby lost at sea?

Asiya – It wasn't my baby. It was never my baby. The problem, Tobi, and I speak from experience, is when we try to see these people as something that they are not.

Tobi I mean, just to play devil's advocate, your family came here under duress.

Asiya The blood of the covenant is thicker than the water of the womb. Have you heard this saying, Tobi? It means that the bonds of shared ideology outweigh the bonds of kinship. The blood that runs through my veins, through due process, documentation, and implicit ideology, is haematically British. Britain once ruled the world. Generations of sacrifice, my ancestors subjugated in the interests of this crumbling empire. And here I am. They suggest I should open the floodgates, hasten its decline? Everywhere you look there are floods and plagues and riots and war. More and more people will appear at these shores. And what is to be done? How can anyone be expected to get on with their day-to-day with babies washing ashore?

Tobi It makes things very difficult.

Asiya Yes. It does.

Beat.

Tobi People like you, Asiya Rao.

Asiya Do they? Really?

Tobi Yes. Definitely. They like you because you're so straight-talking.
   You're not afraid to say the wrong thing.

Asiya I am not afraid.

Tobi You tell it like it is.

Asiya I do.

Tobi What do you really make of this tragedy?

Asiya Every cloud has its silver lining.

Tobi Please. Tell me more.

Asiya People are always referring to the issues we face with migration as a crisis. The Migration Crisis. But I was always taught that where there is crisis there is opportunity. Project Womb is just the beginning. This government seeks to provide the ultimate safety, while adhering to the highest humanitarian standards.

Tobi You referred earlier to a 'practical humanitarianism'.

Asiya Yes. Words, Tobi, must be moulded to fit the prevailing logic. What do we do next? There are no new ideas under the sun. Take those who come through the correct channels and set them up in the outposts. Enforce opportunities for labour. Win-win.

Tobi Uh, how do they win?

Asiya They win the right to exist.

Tobi Of course. And, I mean, why stop there?

Asiya Exactly! Our noble efforts are constantly under attack by riff-raff on all fronts. So-called scholars, so-called fact-checkers, so-called courts. Honestly, some people have nothing better to do with their time. But rest assured we will crack down on this antisocial behaviour. We must protect civility.

Phoebe re-enters the carriage, now alert.

In our brainstorming sessions at the Home Office, we encourage each other to think freely. What are the raw materials at our disposal? What is to be done with the by-products of the wall? With the irradiated masses? Fuel crisis? What fuel crisis? Where you see humans and babies, I see opportunities for clean energy! Babies for biomass. Biofuel. Paddies. Paddy fields. Yes! Why not? Why stop there?

Phoebe This interview is over.

Tobi Thank you. 'Babies for biomass.' That will do nicely.

Phoebe All of that was off the record.

Tobi Yeah, that's not how it works. But I've got what I need.

Phoebe We're not finished.

Tobi Oh, I believe we are. Thank you for this. That was perfection.

We hear the sound of Haben singing in the corridor.

Phoebe You know what. Have your moment. I'll take it up with your editor. Bennet and I are old friends. He won't run this.

Tobi Oh, I don't know about that.

Tobi taps her recording device.

Bennet owes me a favour. Scott was pretty . . . handsy.

Phoebe You're overestimating your leverage. You've had your little day out in the sunshine. Tomorrow you'll be back to writing pieces on queer global fashion icons.

Tobi Omigod. That's it. Number eight.

Phoebe What?
What are you talking about?

Tobi heads to the corridor. She is pursued by Phoebe, and then Asiya.

Asiya stops dead at the sight of Haben cradling baby Momo.

Tobi You're number eight.

Asiya Baby Momo??

Asiya faints once again.

Tobi Asiya!
(*Fanning Asiya awake.*) What's happened? Is she okay?

Phoebe She's fine.
(*Stepping over Asiya.*) But Momo! Momo is awake. What's happened?

Haben Yes. I was just airing my giant bag out the window and lo and behold, Momo . . .

Phoebe (*offering to take the baby*) Here, I can –

Haben (*pulling the baby away protectively*) I think it's best that I keep hold of the baby.

Asiya (*woozily awakening*) The bag is Hermès! Very exclusive. Very exclusive.

Tobi Ah, Hermes. The Ancient Greek god of commerce and trickery.
You're not Manjula Aunty. You're Haben Haile. You were number eight in my piece on queer global fashion icons. 'Haben Haile. She's a triple threat. She can act. She can sing. She can dance. Haben Haile is panache personified. She has recently fled her home country due to threats on her life for being outspoken about her sexuality.'

Haben Leave me out of this. Please.

Tobi You are an asylum seeker. Hired to play the role of the home secretary's mother? For some sort of PR angle? To give a human face to this draconian sea wall –

Asiya – Thermowomb thermowomb –

Tobi But why make such an effort? Could Phoebe Bernays, of the great Bernays family, pioneers of British engineering, have any vested interests in this development?

Haben Tobi. Please. Please leave my name out of your story. It will ruin my case.

Tobi I'm sorry but it's a celebrity angle. This story is going to go big.

Haben You will ruin my life. And for what? These people govern your country. These buffoons. You are telling me that your countrymen need further evidence of their corruption??

Tobi This is it. This is why I came into journalism.

Phoebe Clever little cookie. So much potential. It's a shame.

    BOOM! In one smooth motion, Phoebe shunts Tobi out the window. Now outside the train, she manages to keep a grip on the windowpane.
    There is scope here for a top-of-train chase scene at director's discretion.

Tobi Please! Don't . . .!

    Asiya pries her fingers off the window ledge. A dull thud, then silence. They look at each other or avoid eye contact. Haben rocks the baby. Phoebe begins to type into Tobi's phone furiously.

Asiya (*to Phoebe*) What are you doing?

Phoebe Submitting our story. '*Times on the Train* with Asiya Rao'. Just drafting up the ideal version. God it would be so much easier if we could just cut out the middlemen.
    Let's get rid of this recording.

    Stomps on Tobi's recording device, or deletes file on phone.

Then we'll do the messages. To the nearest and dearest.
Dear Mum, I cannot go on.
I'm sorry.
I will always love you.
Et cetera.
She was a long-term depressive.

Phoebe looks up from her furious typing, to Asiya and Haben.

The line is as follows: The interview concluded at quarter to twelve. Tobi headed to the corridor a couple minutes later. We all heard a thud at five minutes past twelve. We thought nothing of it.

Act Five

5.1

A few minutes later. Haben, Asiya and Phoebe are seated in their original seats. Each looking forward as if nothing happened. Haben cradles the baby.

Conductor (*voice-over*) Ladies and gentlemen, we are currently arriving at London St Pancras, where this train terminates. London St Pancras, our final destination, in a few moments' time.

> *Haben types something into her phone.*
> *The sound of Haben pinging a message to Phoebe.*

Phoebe (*whipping her head around in horror*) What's this?

Haben (*walking back over towards Phoebe*) I took a few photos.
Of our love-making last night.

> *Phoebe goes to grab the phone.*

I've backed them up, of course.

> *Asiya appears more mortified than she has been at any point of this journey.*

Asiya Oh dear. I'm sorry. I am truly mortified. I'll leave you to –

Phoebe What do you want?

Haben I took them. Originally, because the Home Office, your office, prefers photographic evidence of my sexual orientation to support my claim of asylum.
I felt terrible.

> *Beat.*

Given the events of the day, I now feel less terrible.

Phoebe What do you want?

Haben I want every effort to be made to find the mother of this baby. I want a full enquiry to be made into the sinking of that dinghy in the Channel. If any pushbacks were involved, I want justice. If the mother of this baby is no longer with us, I want papers for the baby. I want papers for myself. I want decent accommodation in a mixed area. And I want work. I want a job teaching music to children.

Phoebe Fuck me.

Haben I'd rather not.

Phoebe Fine. I'll see to it.

    Phoebe and Haben shake hands.
    Haben prepares to exit, lovingly cradling baby Moses.

Conductor (*voice-over*) We are now arriving at London St Pancras where this train terminates. Please make sure you take all your belongings with you as you leave the train.

Asiya All's well that ends well.

Phoebe A few minor hiccups. But we're back on track. I'm going to recalibrate your speech on account of the incident of the Channel. I need you on top form. Are you on top form?

Asiya (*adjusting*) I'm on top form. Thatcher. Napoleon. Beyoncé.

    The train arrives in St Pancras station.
    Tobi climbs down from the open doors. She is battered and wind-blown, but very much alive. Tobi points at Phoebe. Laughing manically:

Tobi You! You're going to pay for this. What a gift. What a story . . . I mean yesterday, I was ranking matte lipsticks, and today I'm going to write the story that single-handedly brings down this administration.

Phoebe Are you, though?

Tobi What are you going to do? Chuck me off the train again? We're in the station.

Phoebe Tobi, I'm just worried that with your history . . .

Tobi What history?

Phoebe Your extensive history of anxiety and depression. That you may be having some sort of episode.

Tobi . . . Where's my phone?

Phoebe There is no longer any evidence of our interview. You must have deleted it. During your little episode in the corridor.

Tobi What episode?

Phoebe You have two options. You can attempt to run this story. We will defame you, discredit your character, and if it comes to it, we will prosecute you under the Official Secrets Act.

Tobi This is in the public interest.

Phoebe The act has been extended to cover a very wide range of information deemed damaging to the interests of the state. We have the finest lawyers in the country. And you have . . .? Bennet, I assure you, will not back you on this one.

Tobi Then I'll take the story elsewhere.

Phoebe We're talking a lengthy legal process, that we are certain to win. With your history, I'd worry you 'just wouldn't be the same' after all that. Our reputation managers are the best of the best. Would anyone believe you? Alongside some choice details about your erratic past, there will be the insinuation of fabrication. The last thing any journalist wants.

Tobi You can't silence me.

Phoebe No. In fact. I want the opposite. I want to amplify your voice.

Tobi Aye right.

Phoebe I'm looking for a new director of communications. You may have some minor grievances with me, but with that on your CV you can have any job in the world that you desire. The world opens to you. Everything becomes possible. You want to start your own publication? You'll have investors breaking down your door. A beautiful office overlooking the Thames. Fresh lilies every morning in a glass vase. No more puff pieces to pay the bills. You could clear your debt with your first pay cheque. I know you believe in change. Think of how much you could achieve for humanity.

Beat.

Are you interested?

Tobi hesitates, then:

Tobi (*fixing her hair*) I might be.

Phoebe Good. Then stay where I can see you. We have a press conference to attend.

Beat.

Oh, and you might want to text your mum.

Tobi What?

Phoebe Tell her you decided to choose life.

5.2

Press conference at the Project Womb test rig. Buzzing and murmuring. The staircases from 1.1 in a different configuration. Perhaps Phoebe, Tobi and Asiya all wear hard hats. Asiya ascends the platform. She addresses the audience. She is engaging, charismatic, likeable.

Asiya Thank you all for coming here today. I'm sure we can all agree that these are extraordinary times. Just this morning I was in Dover. As I stood with two feet in the Channel, a shiver ran down my spine. I felt a dark, lurking presence in the water. Make no mistake, we are a nation under siege. The illegals invading our coastline are a threat to our livelihoods, our prosperity, our way of life.

Now, there is no question that what happened today in the Channel is a tragedy. As you know, I'm a family woman myself, and thus was deeply and personally affected.

I have a dream of returning this country to its former, sovereign glory. Of stamping out the dark and murky pools and stopping dissent before it starts.

We are building a new economy based on security. Advanced military technologies. Surveillance drones. Razor wire. The migration crisis has presented tremendous opportunities for investment, separating those who have the right to exist from those who do not. Project Womb is the ultimate safety. And without any further ado, let's have a little taste, shall we?

Flicks the switch. Nothing happens.

Voices: Is it plugged in? Try switching it on and off. Ah. It begins to work. Enclosure. The audience has a feeling of being enclosed. Pink. Some mechanical noises.

Project Womb represents everything this party stands for. It symbolises the direction we are heading as a nation. We have coined the new slogan: 'Let's Look Inwards.' We will enclose ourselves in our independence. Incarcerate our freedom. Thrive in a cellule of our own sovereignty.

A fish flops onstage and dies.

This is a legacy project, and my crowning achievement at the Home Office. It is on the back of this historic development that I would like to announce my candidacy for party leadership. Thank you. Thank you very much.

This afternoon I took a largely uneventful train journey from the coast of Dover. It gave me a chance to reflect. As I gazed wistfully out the window, I dreamt of the clouds and the stars and the skies, and the sea as it rises and falls. I thought of how at the end of the day we are isolated and alone. Everything that we love will leave us. If you love something. You must enclose it in a wall. Be it a wall of bricks and mortar or walls of ionising radiation. You must seal it off entirely so that it never grows or changes. Ever.

As I sat on that train. I began to use my imagination.

We hear the singing of children.
The laughter of a baby.

Momo?

Sorry. I imagined a world where . . . I imagined . . . I imagined . . .

Together Let's Look Inwards. Inwards into the void.

Something cracks. The water breaks. Our final image is Haben as the new Britannia, teaching music to children. Momo glows.

Projections near Haben show images of hostility and images of humanity and resistance: Kenmure Street, perhaps German Jews being turned back from seeking asylum in the UK during World War Two, hostile environment 'Go Home' vans, Berliners welcoming Ukrainian refugees at the train station, acts of kindness and joy, community events with dancing, Kill the Bill demos and so on. The actors perhaps remove their costumes and watch.

Chants, preferably real recordings: 'Whose streets? Our streets.'

We hear the rumblings.

The End.